THE ART OF
WILLIAM BLAKE

NUMBER *12*

BAMPTON LECTURES IN AMERICA

DELIVERED AT COLUMBIA UNIVERSITY

1959

THE ART OF

WILLIAM

BLAKE

BY ANTHONY BLUNT

ICON EDITIONS
HARPER & ROW, PUBLISHERS
NEW YORK, EVANSTON, SAN FRANCISCO, LONDON

This book was first published by Columbia University Press and is herewith reprinted by arrangement.

THE ART OF WILLIAM BLAKE. Copyright © 1959 by Columbia University Press. All rights reserved. Printed in the United States of America. No part of this book may be used or reproduced in any manner whatsoever without written permission except in the case of brief quotations embodied in critical articles and reviews. For information address Harper & Row, Publishers, Inc., 10 East 53rd Street, New York, N.Y. 10022. Published simultaneously in Canada by Fitzhenry & Whiteside Limited, Toronto.

FIRST ICON EDITION 1974.

ISBN 0-06-430045-5

Acknowledgements

THE AUTHOR wishes to thank the following owners for permission to reproduce works in their possession: the Trustees of the British Museum for Plates 1, 3b, 5a, 10c, 11b, 13a, 20a and b, 21a and b, 23a, 29a and b, 30b, 41c, 44, 46a, 54b, 55a, 62, and 64a; the Trustees of the Tate Gallery for Plates 4a, 8a, 26a and b, 28a and b, 30c, 31c, 32b, 33, 34a, 36a and b, 38b, 46c and d, 57c, 58a and b, 61a, 63; the Director of the Victoria and Albert Museum for Plates 6c, 7c, and 35a; the Trustees of the Sir John Soane's Museum for Plate 16b; the Corporation of Birmingham for Plate 60a; the University of Oxford for Plates 24b and 42c; the Syndics of the Fitzwilliam Museum, Cambridge, for Plates 8c, 13c, 21c, 32c, 37a; the Royal Society of Arts for Plate 8d; the Society of Antiquaries of London for Plate 2a; the Whitworth Institute of Manchester for Plate 24a; the Provost and Fellows of New College, Oxford, for Plate 64b; His Grace the Archbishop of Canterbury and the Trustees of Lambeth Palace Library for Plate 54c; the Dean and Chapter of Winchester for Plate 39b; the National Gallery of Victoria, Melbourne (Felton Bequest) for Plate 59a; the Director of the Kunsthaus, Zurich, for Plates 11c, 27b, 40c and 57a; the Museum of Fine Arts, Boston, for Plates 9d, 40a and b, 45, 46b, and 47; the Henry E. Huntington Library and Art Gallery, San Marino, California, for Plate 11a; the Pierpont Morgan Library, New York, for Plate 56b; the Fogg Art Museum, Harvard University, Grenville Lindall Winthrop Collection, for Plates 39a and 60b; the Brooklyn Museum, New York, for Plate 38a; the Dowager Lady Aberconway for Plate 57b; Mr. George Goyder for Plates 34b and 42a; and Sir Geoffrey Keynes for Plates 3a and 12c.

Preface

THIS BOOK is the outcome of an invitation from Columbia University to deliver the Bampton Lectures there in 1959, and, apart from small alterations and the addition of two appendices, the text is that prepared for this purpose. I have made no attempt to convert the lectures into a full-dress monograph, because a short course of lectures in fact offered me exactly the scale that I wanted. My ambition has not been to write an exhaustive study of Blake as an artist but to provide a general introduction to his art. I have not, therefore, attempted to deal with the many problems of chronology, derivation, and meaning which offer themselves on every side, and have tried rather to give an account of Blake's ideas on the nature of art and to see how far he achieved his aims as an artist. As Blake's paintings and engravings are intended primarily to express his religious and philosophical ideas, it is impossible to discuss the former without to some extent examining the latter, but I have tried to summarise his doctrines without becoming involved in the details of his complex system of mystical symbolism.

As an artist and as a poet Blake is an unusual phenomenon, but it is part of my aim in this book to show that he is not so unique as is often maintained. He had much in common with certain of his contemporaries, and learned much from his predecessors. Indeed it could be said that he was one of the most traditional of thinkers and painters in that he drew unashamedly on the ideas and images which had been accumulated before his own time. To say this is not, however, in any way to diminish his originality. His imagination was so powerful that he could never be seduced into imitation, and his mind was so original that it could only be enriched by learning from others.

The study of Blake has been bedevilled by uncontrolled enthusiasm and disproportionate praise. He has been described as a more imaginative painter than Michelangelo, and a more skilful engraver than Dürer. Such statements are foolish and tend only to conceal his real merits, which are so great and so rare that they are not obscured by admitting his weaknesses.

A vast quantity of energy and an excessive amount of ingenuity have gone into the study of Blake in the last twenty years. His philosophy and theology have been analysed to the last hair; his sources have been studied *ad nauseam;* his simplest poems have been made the basis for mountains of exegesis; but little has been written about Blake as a painter and an engraver. Moreover, most of what has been written has been directed towards the symbolism of the designs, and they have been considered simply for the light they may throw on the poems. The ordinary methods of art history have never been applied to Blake. No general account has been given of the sources of his style, of his relation to his contemporaries' painting, or of his development as an artist. If the known facts are put together, they furnish a picture of an artist who, though endowed with unusual gifts, yet fits in more than might be expected with the ordinary pattern of artistic behaviour.

In the preparation of this book I have incurred many debts to others. First I must express my gratitude to the authorities of Columbia University for inviting me to participate in the great series of Bampton Lectures; to Professor and Mrs. Rudolf Wittkower for their help and kindness before and during the course; and to the members of the staff and the student body of Columbia who braved the weather and other obstacles to form the most stimulating and appreciative audience that it has been my privilege to address.

The preparation of the final text would have been impossible without the help of Miss Elsa Scheerer, who has at all stages helped in tedious matters such as checking references, compiling the bibliography, and correcting proofs, and whose attention to detail has eliminated many inaccuracies and inconsistencies. Finally I must thank the staff of the Columbia University Press for the rare combination of rapidity and patience which they have displayed in seeing the book through the press.

Anthony Blunt

London, England
July, 1959

Contents

THE ART OF
WILLIAM BLAKE

1. Blake's Early Years

BLAKE'S DEVELOPMENT as a painter was the exact opposite to his evolution as a poet. By the age of twenty he had written some of the finest lyrics in the English language, and as pure poetry he never wrote anything to surpass them in his later life. As a painter, if he had died at the age of thirty he would hardly be remembered at all. At most he would be thought of as a minor and rather incompetent member of a group of artists in revolt against Sir Joshua Reynolds and the official doctrine of the Royal Academy. Moreover, when his genius first began to bear fruit in the visual arts, it was in a field closely linked with his literary work, in the illustration of his poems, such as the *Songs of Innocence,* printed in 1789. In painting, as opposed to decoration added to a written text, he produced nothing of note till the great series of so-called colour-printed drawings which date from 1795. From that time onwards, however, he was to grow steadily in strength as an artist, working up to the great climax of the last years in the illuminations to *Jerusalem,* the engravings to the Book of Job, and the Dante water-colours.

The fact that Blake had little natural facility as a painter and that not only many of his early works but also some of his later ones are clumsy has led critics to maintain that painting was for him a minor activity, and that his works in this medium are altogether inferior to those in poetry or prose. This view is, I believe, false. Painting and poetry were for Blake equally valid means of expressing his ideas—or his visions, to use his own language—and in the Prophetic Books, produced by his special method of illuminated printing, the decorations and illustrations are as significant as the text, sometimes indeed containing ideas which are not brought out in the poem itself. In fact it would be possible to maintain that in his later years Blake's paintings are artistically more successful than his poems, which, though they are effective as vehicles for expressing his doctrines, are often as poetry vague, turgid, and shapeless.[1]

It is my purpose in this book to trace Blake's gradual mastery of the problems of the visual arts, and to show how single-minded was his pursuit of the technical methods and the formal inventions which would most precisely convey the ideas which he had in his mind. For, though Blake was in the highest degree original, both technically and formally, his inventions in both fields were never made for their own sake but only as means to more complete and perfect expression.

The story of Blake's early training as an artist is soon told. In 1767, at the age of ten, he was sent to a drawing school in the Strand, kept by Henry Pars, brother of the better-known William Pars, who about this time was sent to Ionia by the Dilettanti Society to draw the remains of Greek sculpture and architecture. He returned with his portfolio full of drawings, which the young Blake may possibly have been able to study. In any case we know that he drew from casts after the antique, both in Pars' school and from examples which his father bought for him. It would also have been normal for him to copy engravings and drawings, and he certainly began to collect the former on his own initiative at a very early age.

In 1772 the young Blake entered on the second stage of his artistic education and was apprenticed for seven years to the engraver, James

[1] I am aware that this is an old-fashioned view now heretical in Blake circles.

Basire.[2] Basire was a successful, competent, and somewhat old-fashioned engraver who ran a large establishment to supply publishers with engravings, many of which were partly or wholly executed by his apprentices, although they bear the name of Basire as the master of the *bottega*. Blake learned from Basire a severe technique of engraving which was opposed to the more flashy style introduced from Italy by Bartolozzi and others, but in the end it suited Blake's purpose better, because its sharpness enabled him to give his engraved line that wiry quality which he sought in his mature works. Basire was connected with the illustrations to Stuart's *The Antiquities of Athens,* so that in his studio Blake would, as at Pars', have come under the influence of the neoclassical movement; but much more important from the point of view of his later development was the fact that his master was engaged on the illustrations to Richard Gough's *Sepulchral Monuments of Great Britain,* the preparatory drawings for which were largely entrusted to Blake.[3] The result of this commission was that he spent a great part of his time as apprentice with Basire in the solemn atmosphere of Westminster Abbey, making drawings of the monuments to the mediaeval kings and queens of England. Some of these he also engraved for Gough's volumes, and the best of them, such as the *Edward III,* the *Queen Philippa,* and the *Aveline of Lancaster* (Plate 2*b*), prove his technical skill;[4] but

[2] Cf. Keynes, *Blake Studies,* p. 41.

[3] According to Gilchrist (*Life of Blake,* p. 12), Blake also engraved some of the plates which bear the name of Basire in the early volumes of *Archaeologia* and *Vetusta Monumenta,* publications of the Society of Antiquaries, and in the *Memoirs* of Thomas Hollis. Those in the second volume of *Vetusta Monumenta* include several of tombs and paintings in Westminster Abbey clearly by Blake.

[4] These are the plates specifically ascribed to him by Gilchrist, but on style it is safe to add those illustrating the heads of Henry III and Richard II and of their queens, which are in precisely the same manner. At the same time Blake probably made the water-colour copies (Plate 2*a*) of the wall-paintings of two English kings in Westminster Abbey (called Henry III and King Sebert) which now belong to the Society of Antiquaries and which are engraved in the second volume of *Vetusta Monumenta.*

the importance of this commission was that it gave him his first contact
with mediaeval art, which was to remain a powerful influence and source
of inspiration for the whole of his life.

One other engraving (Plate 3a) executed in 1773 at the beginning of
his apprenticeship with Basire provides the first evidence of his admiration
for Michelangelo, another continuing source of inspiration for him.
The engraving in its original state is a copy of the figure in the lower
right-hand corner of Michelangelo's *Martyrdom of St. Peter* in the
Pauline Chapel.[5] According to the inscription in Blake's own hand on
the unique copy of the first state, the engraving was made after a drawing
by Salviati from Michelangelo. This drawing has not been identified, and
the attribution to Salviati may not have been correct, but it indicates
that at this time Blake studied not only engravings after Italian masters
of the sixteenth century, which would have been easily accessible to him,
but also drawings of the school of Michelangelo. Confirmation of this
connection is to be found in two drawings[6] in which the artist uses precisely the system of cross-hatching to be found in the drawings of Daniele
da Volterra and his followers.

There is enough evidence to define Blake's style about the time that he
left Basire's shop. One water-colour, the *Penance of Jane Shore* (Plate
4a), can be assigned to the last years of his apprenticeship.[7] The engraving

[5] At a later date Blake reworked the plate, emphasising the outlines, inserting the date
of the original state, 1773, and adding an inscription describing the figure as Joseph of
Arimathea. The first state is reproduced by Keynes in *Blake Studies*, Plate 14.

[6] One is reproduced here on Plate 3b, the other by Sir Geoffrey Keynes (*Pencil Drawings*, Plate 3, and *Blake Studies*, p. 7), who has suggested that this drawing may be a
study made from Blake's brother Robert, but there does not seem to be any conclusive
evidence for this view. An alternative hypothesis is that the drawing may have been made
from the living model when Blake was a student at the Royal Academy in 1779. For the
pose of the drawing with the unusual combination of the outstretched right arm and
the left arm bent with the hand to the breast, cf. a drawing by Daniele da Volterra at
Windsor (A. Popham and J. Wilde, *Italian Drawings at Windsor Castle*, London, 1949,
No. 263, Plate 77).

[7] In the *Descriptive Catalogue* to the exhibition of 1809 Blake states that this painting

Edward and Eleanor (Plate 5a) was executed soon after he left his master,[8] and a rough sketch of the *Death of Earl Godwin* was made in preparation for a painting exhibited in the Royal Academy in 1780.[9] On stylistic grounds we may safely add to this group certain other works: the *Ordeal of Queen Emma* [10] (Plate 4b), the *Keys of Calais*,[11] and a water-colour belonging to Mr. Harold Macmillan, the subject of which has been identified as *Saul and David* or *Joash*,[12] but which probably represents a scene from English mediaeval history, such as Edward III presenting the Black Prince to the barons as Prince of Wales.[13]

It is in fact clear, as Gilchrist pointed out, that at this date Blake must

---

was "done above Thirty Years ago" (*Works*, ed. by Keynes, p. 806). The preparatory drawing for the painting in the collection of Sir Geoffrey Keynes is reproduced in his *Blake's Pencil Drawings: Second Series*, Plate 1.

[8] Cf. Gilchrist, *Life of Blake*, p. 26, and Keynes, *Separate Plates*, p. 17.

[9] Cf. Gilchrist, *Life of Blake*, p. 29. The sketch is now in the collection of Mr. George Goyder.

[10] Formerly in the Graham Robertson Collection (Preston, *The Blake Collection of W. Graham Robertson*, p. 167).

[11] Formerly in the Graham Robertson Collection (*ibid.*, p. 174).

[12] Cf. Keynes, *Illustrations to the Bible*, No. 56.

[13] Alternatively the painting may represent a scene in Blake's own fragment of *Edward III* in which the king knights his son before setting off for the French War. Blake's drawing of a youth springing up from a hill side, made in 1780 and later used for the print known as *Glad Day*, probably also illustrates a passage from this play in which on the morning of the battle of Crécy Lord Audley greets Sir Thomas Dagworth with the words:

> The bright morn
> Smiles on our army, and the gallant sun
> Springs from the hill like a young hero
> Into the battle, shaking his golden locks
> Exultingly.   (*Works*, p. 25)

The engraving itself bears the inscription *WB inv 1780* and is generally said to have been engraved in that year, but there seems good reason to believe Sir Geoffrey Keynes' theory that only the preparatory drawing (in the Victoria and Albert Museum) was made at that time and that the engraving itself was executed much later, when the ideas embodied in the inscription at the bottom of the plate were already fully developed in Blake's mind. If this is so, the coloured version which is printed from the same plate was probably made at the same time as the line-engraving. The case of the *Joseph of Arimathea* (cf. p. 4, note 5) shows that the inscriptions on Blake's engravings can be misleading.

have been planning a series of illustrations to the early history of England, a subject which he also treated in various fragments of plays in the *Poetical Sketches* composed during the same years.[14] In choosing mediaeval English subjects Blake was not alone, for other painters were treating similar themes at the same time. In the Academy of 1776, for instance, Edward Penny had exhibited a painting of the *Penance of Jane Shore*,[15] but the real specialists in this type of theme were Angelica Kauffmann and John Hamilton Mortimer, for the latter of whom Blake had a great admiration. The works of both these artists in this particular field are preserved mainly in engravings (cf. Plate 5*b*), but it is clear from these that neither of them made any attempt to dress their figures in correct mediaeval costume or to give a Gothic character to the scene as a whole. In costume they followed contemporary stage productions of Shakespeare or plays dealing with mediaeval themes, which consisted of a mixture of Elizabethan and eighteenth-century elements with the occasional addition of a mediaeval suit of armour rendered with considerable freedom. For the setting a couple of Gothic arches in the background served as a reminder that the scene took place in the Middle Ages. The style employed for the drawing of figures and draperies was the current manner, on the borderline between late Rococo and neoclassicism, employed by Angelica Kauffmann equally for Gothic, Greek, or contemporary subjects. A comparison between her *Edward and Eleanor* and Blake's version of the same subject is enough to establish the difference between their attitudes toward the Middle Ages.

Mortimer made a slightly more serious attempt to create a mediaeval

[14] For example, *King Edward the Third*, *King Edward the Fourth*, and *King John*. Blake's principal source appears to have been Rapin, who in his *History of England* tells the stories of Queen Emma, Earl Godwin, Edward and Eleanor, the Keys of Calais, and Edward III making his son, the Black Prince, Prince of Wales. He may also have taken some ideas from Camden's *Britannia* (e.g. the story of Edward and Eleanor, which, according to Rapin, is first recorded by Camden).

[15] No. 221.

atmosphere, and in paintings such as *Magna Carta* he comes closer to Blake than any other of his contemporaries; but, generally speaking, he employs the current idiom.[16] His *Battle of Agincourt* is in the manner of the much admired Giulio Romano, and his *Vortigern and Rowena* (Plate 41*b*) suggests the eighteenth-century idea of an oriental harem rather than the court of an Anglo-Saxon king.[17]

Blake's representations of mediaeval England are in many ways naïve and in almost all respects inaccurate, but they have a certain conviction and they reveal in their atmosphere the effect of his studies in Westminster Abbey. In *Jane Shore* he employs the mixed costume favoured by Angelica Kauffmann and Mortimer, but generally his costumes have a more mediaeval flavour. The background of the *Queen Emma* is in a

[16] Paintings of English mediaeval subjects exhibited at the Royal Academy during the 1770s include the following:

1769 Samuel Wale, *St. Austin Preaching* (117), *The Widow of King Edward IV and the Duke of York* (118).

1770 Angelica Kauffmann, *Vortigern and Rowena* (116).

1771 Angelica Kauffmann, *Edgar and Elfrida* (113); Samuel Wale, *King Alfred Making a Code of Laws* (208).

1772 Edward Penny, *Rosamund and Queen Eleanor* (192); Samuel Wale, *The Wife of Perkin Warbeck before Henry VII* (268).

1773 Benjamin West, *The Death of Bayard* (305).

1774 William Hamilton, *Edgar and Elfrida* (114); Samuel Wale, *St. Augustine Preaching* (309).

1776 Angelica Kauffmann, *Edward and Eleanor* (155), *Lady Elizabeth Grey and Edward IV* (156); Samuel Wale, *The Citizens of London Swearing Allegiance to William I* (311), *The Widow of Edward IV and the Duke of York* (312).

1778 Thomas Burgess, *William I Dismounted by His Eldest Son* (29); Benjamin West, *William de Albanac Presents His Daughter to Alfred* (331).

1779 Josiah Boydell, *William de Albanac Presents His Daughter to Alfred* (23); John Mortimer, *The Battle of Agincourt* (203), *The Meeting of Vortigern and Rowena* (204); Benjamin West, *Alfred Divides His Loaf with a Pilgrim* (341).

The paintings by Mortimer exhibited in 1779 were all painted earlier (from 1770 onwards), but were included in the exhibition of that year because of his election to the Academy.

[17] This unusual subject seems to have been popularised by Camden and Rapin; it occurs in an engraving of 1752 by Nicholas Blakey and in a drawing by Fuseli of 1769 (cf. Schiff, *Zeichnungen von J. H. Füssli*, p. 4).

style some centuries later than the date of the subject, and even as a rendering of late Gothic architecture it can hardly be considered accurate; but the draperies, with their pointed folds, are clearly based on models such as the tomb of Aveline of Lancaster in Westminster Abbey (Plate 2*b*), which Blake must certainly have known.[18]

This genuine interest in mediaeval sculpture and the attempt to imitate the style of the Westminster tombs in painting were unusual in England in the 1770s. Horace Walpole and others had, of course, instigated an enthusiasm for the Middle Ages, but it was of a primarily romantic kind and did not involve a careful study of the actual style of mediaeval art. At Strawberry Hill Walpole could mix details from mediaeval architecture with *chinoiserie* motives without any sense of incongruity, on the grounds that both Gothic and Chinese cultures were for him something remote and fantastic which served as an escape from the polished classical culture of Augustan England. To Blake the tombs of Westminster Abbey had an entirely different meaning; they represented true art as opposed to all the artificial styles which were current in his day. Just as the fragments of plays in the *Poetical Sketches* had a genuine flavour of the Elizabethan if not of the Plantagenet era, so Blake's early water-colours of English history caught something of the heroic atmosphere of a past era which was missed by his contemporaries.

Given the small number of paintings surviving from this series illustrating English history, it would be unwise to deduce any firm conclusions about Blake's intentions, but it is worth noticing that many of them illustrate themes with which Blake was to be much concerned in later years. The *Death of Earl Godwin,* for instance, illustrates divine vengeance on murderers. The earl was suspected of having murdered the brother of Edward the Confessor, and while dining with the king he swore to his innocence and added: "I pray God that this morsel . . . may choke me,

[18] See Plates XXIX–XXXI of the second volume of *Vetusta Monumenta.*

if I had any hand in the death of that prince," upon which he ate it and choked.[19] The *Keys of Calais,* showing Queen Philippa of Hainaut pleading with Edward III to spare the lives of the burghers, teaches the quality of mercy.[20] *Edward and Eleanor,* in which the queen sucks the poison from the wound of Prince Edward, later Edward I, at the Siege of Acre, is a theme of self-sacrifice and heroism.[21]

Two of the paintings are, however, even more closely related to Blake's personal views than these: *Jane Shore* and *Queen Emma,* which deal with the hypocrisy of established religion and conventional morality over sexual matters. Queen Emma, according to the legend, was wrongly accused by her son Edward the Confessor of unchastity and proved her innocence by demanding to be subjected to the ordeal by fire, the scene shown in Blake's water-colour.[22] Jane Shore, the mistress of Edward IV, a woman of great intelligence and generosity, was after his death subjected to every indignity by Richard III, and having been publicly declared a harlot by the Bishop of London, was made to do penance at St. Paul's, which is the theme of Blake's painting.[23] The hypothesis that Blake chose this story as an example of hypocrisy in sexual matters is confirmed by the entry in the Royal Academy catalogue for Penny's painting of the same subject: "The insolent in office, and pretenders to purity, by insulting the wretched, betray their own baseness."

On leaving Basire's studio in 1779, Blake enrolled as a student at the Royal Academy School. His short stay there was, as we can gather from his own statements, unsatisfactory. It was at this time that he formed his violent dislike of Sir Joshua Reynolds, and his relations with the Keeper, Moser, were no better. Moser immediately put himself out of court

[19] Rapin, *History of England,* II, 75.   [20] *Ibid.,* IV, 273.
[21] *Ibid.,* III, 489.   [22] *Ibid.,* II, 64.
[23] The story of Jane Shore had been popularised by Nicholas Rowe, whose play, first produced in 1714, was frequently revived throughout the eighteenth century. Mrs. Siddons, who acted the title role in 1782, was twice painted in it by William Hamilton (Victoria and Albert Museum and Nettlefold Collection).

with Blake by telling him to study engravings after Lebrun and Rubens, instead of Raphael and Michelangelo.[24] Blake must, however, have learned something at the School, where he continued to copy the antique and, probably for the first time, drew from the life.

For the years immediately following Blake's short period at the Royal Academy School there is very little information. An elegant frontispiece to Commins' *Elegy Set to Music,* drawn and engraved in 1782 (Plate 12*a*), shows him working in a fashionable idiom not far removed from that of Stothard. But it was at about this time that he first began to illustrate two authors who were to occupy him greatly in later life: Shakespeare and Milton. The water-colour of *Oberon, Titania and Puck* and the small sketch of *Lear and Cordelia* (Plate 8*a*), both in the Tate Gallery, must date from these years, and a drawing of *Adam and Eve Sleeping,* in the collection of Mrs. Bateson, though usually dated to 1808, must be assigned to the same years.[25] For the figure of Cordelia the artist seems to have turned once more to a drawing by or after Daniele da Volterra, such as one in the collection of the late Sir Robert Mond,[26] the pose of which is also close to the Eve in the *Adam and Eve Sleeping.*

In the year following the purely conventional frontispiece to Commins Blake began to develop some of the characteristics which are normally associated with his mature style. Certain true Blake figures begin to appear, notably the white-bearded old man who later was to play the part of Job, Jehovah, and Urizen; and at the same time the artist begins to use forms which are intended to express grandeur, but which at this stage are often somewhat inflated and empty.[27]

Once again we can point to a contemporary artist as a powerful in-

[24] *Works,* p. 975.

[25] Reproduced in Keynes, *Pencil Drawings,* Plate 35. The authenticity of this drawing is somewhat doubtful, and it has been attributed by Mr. Erdman to Edward Burney.

[26] T. Borenius and R. Wittkower, *Catalogue of Collection of Sir Robert Mond* (London, 1937), p. 213.

[27] Drawings and water-colours of this type are as follows: *Samuel and the Witch of Endor,* dated 1783 (New York Public Library); *Abraham and Isaac,* dated 1783 (Museum

fluence on Blake during this phase: James Barry. The same elegant but somewhat empty forms to be seen in Blake's paintings are to be found, for instance, in Barry's paintings in the Royal Society of Arts, begun in 1777 (Plate 8*d*); and the shaggy, bearded old men have close parallels in Barry's and Mortimer's engravings of Lear, one of which (Plate 9*b*) Blake almost copied in a series of six small water-colours of Shakespearian subjects in the Museum of Fine Arts, Boston (Plate 9*d*). Blake moreover, frequently refers to Barry in his writings and cites him as one of the great examples of the neglect with which imaginative artists are always treated by the English.[28] The finest works of this early phase of Blake's art are the water-colour and engraving of *Job's Complaint* (Plate 9*a*), which probably date from about 1786. Here we see not only technical skill, but something of that prophetic solemnity characteristic of Blake's later works.[29]

Although Blake did not produce any works of startling originality in

of Fine Arts, Boston); the various versions of the *Breach in a City,* one of which was exhibited in the Royal Academy in 1784 (No. 27, Plate 8*b*); *Elijah and Elisha* (George Goyder); *Lot and the Angels* (Auckland Public Library); three paintings of the story of Joseph, exhibited (Nos. 449, 455, 462) in the Royal Academy in 1785 (Fitzwilliam Museum, Cambridge), and two sketches from them (Royal Library, Windsor); the *Spirit of the Just Man Newly Departed* (Royal Library, Windsor); *Job and His Family* (John J. Warrington Collection, lent to the Cincinnati Art Museum; No. 57 in Keynes, *Illustrations to the Bible*); possibly one version of *The Plague* (*ibid.*, No. 38a); and six small oval water-colours of Shakespearean scenes (Museum of Fine Arts, Boston).

[28] He proposed his name as one of the artists capable of painting memorial frescoes of great men (*Works,* p. 84). He attacked the Society for the Encouragement of the Arts for their failure to reward him adequately for his paintings in their Great Room (*ibid.,* p. 971). He planned a poem called *Barry,* of which the only surviving fragment is a violent attack on Reynolds (*ibid.,* p. 1018). When in reading the *Discourses* of Sir Joshua Reynolds he finds a passage with which he agrees, he writes in the margin: "Somebody else wrote this page for Reynolds. I think Barry or Fuseli wrote it, or dictated it" (*ibid.,* p. 994).

[29] The preliminary drawing for the *Job* (Tate Gallery; Butlin, *Catalogue,* No. 5), though very crude, has a sort of energy lacking in most of Blake's early works. The same manner appears in the *Robinson Crusoe* (Birmingham), and in three drawings of a subject sometimes called *The Good Farmer,* sometimes the *Bread of Life,* of which versions are in the Tate, the British Museum, and in the J. Schwartz Collection. The style of the water-colour and the engraving of *Job* is repeated in the designs for *Tiriel* of 1789.

painting or engraving before 1789—the date of the *Songs of Innocence*—he had taken up a quite definite position in relation to the various movements going on around him. In poetry he had set his face against the Augustans and turned for inspiration to the Elizabethans, reading with enthusiasm not only the plays but the poems of Shakespeare. Among his own contemporaries his favourites were Gray, Collins, and Thomson, and he admired both Chatterton and Macpherson, whose forgeries he took at their face value,[30] and he studied Percy's *Reliques* with enthusiasm. In philosophy he read Bacon, Locke, and Voltaire and hated them, together with the whole body of rationalist and materialist philosophy; but in spite of this he was a strong Radical, a supporter of the American Revolution, and a friend of Paine, Godwin and the circle of left-wing enthusiasts who met at the house of Joseph Johnson. In the field of art he had sided, as we have seen, with Mortimer and Barry against Sir Joshua Reynolds and the Royal Academy, and about the same time he was to become a close personal friend of Fuseli and Flaxman. In fact he had thrown in his lot with those poets and painters who were preparing the way for the Romantic movement. His *Poetical Sketches* look forward to the *Lyrical Ballads,* which were not published till fifteen years later, and, though his paintings and engravings were not so original, they gave the finest expression to certain ideas which were current in advanced circles in England about this time.

[30] Cf. *Works*, 1025.

2. Blake and the Sublime

THE CONCEPT of the sublime played a great part first in literary and then in artistic criticism during the eighteenth century; but the term was used in different senses by different writers. We are not here concerned with the various applications of the word in literary criticism, but in order to understand Blake's position something must be said about its use in connection with the visual arts.

Basically the term goes back to Longinus. For him the sublime is what carries the hearer to "ecstacy"; it is based on the "marvellous" and its "power to amaze." The sublime acts "like a lightning flash"; by it the soul is filled with "joy and exultation." The sublime "reveals at a stroke and in its entirety, the power of the orator," and Longinus would no doubt have said the same of the artist. His treatise on the sublime was given new popularity in the seventeenth century by the translation and commentary of Boileau, but the first writers to apply the term to painting and sculpture do not really follow him closely.

For Anton Raphael Mengs, who was the first to develop the theory systematically, the sublime consisted of a combination of the human and the divine. In his account of the history of Greek art he shows how, in the earlier stages, artists selected what was best in the human types which they saw around them and so arrived at an ideal human beauty. Then, he goes on, "at last they found the degree of medium between the deity and humanity; they united these two parts and thus invented the form of their heroes. Then it was that the art arrived to the most sublime degree." [1] As examples of the sublime he chooses the *Belvedere Torso,* the *Apollo Belvedere,* and Phidias' statues of Athena at Elis and in the Parthenon. [2] For Mengs none of the moderns is sublime: Raphael fails because he is too human and naturalistic and so misses the divine element; Michelangelo is not sublime, he is "terrible" and "extravagant." [3] Barry, who was much influenced by Mengs, follows his principles with slight variations. In his description of the sublime he defines it as the expression of a great mind through physical beauty, which is little more than a Platonic variant of Mengs' definition. [4] In his examples, both positive and negative, he follows Mengs precisely, but in view of other doctrines of the sublime current at the time it is interesting to note that he deliberately excludes writings like the Edda and Hebrew works like the Book of Revelation from the category of sublimity. To him they are "barbarous, disorderly, and . . . Gothic monsters." [5]

Somewhat surprisingly Reynolds' conception of the sublime is nearer to Longinus than to Barry and Mengs. He is practically quoting Longinus when he writes, "the sublime impresses the mind at once with one great idea; it is a single blow: the elegant, indeed, may be produced by repetition; by an accumulation of many minute circumstances." [6] As one would expect, given this difference of definition, the examples of the sublime quoted by Reynolds are also different: Homer and Michelangelo.

Even before Mengs, Barry, and Reynolds were writing, Burke had expounded a totally opposed idea of the sublime in his *Philosophical Enquiry into the Origin of our Ideas of the Sublime and the Beautiful,* first published in 1757. [7] The essential difference between Burke's ideas and

---

[1] *Works of Mengs,* I, 34.   [2] *Ibid.,* II, 62.   [3] *Ibid.*
[4] *Works of Barry,* Vol. 1, 263.   [5] *Ibid.,* II, 239.
[6] Cf. the fourth discourse delivered in 1771 (Reynolds, *The Discourses,* p. 45).
[7] For a full discussion of this work and its position in English literary criticism, see the edition by J. T. Boulton (London, 1958).

those of the writers just mentioned is that for them the sublime is really a superior form of the beautiful, whereas for Burke the two ideas are opposed and mutually exclusive. Burke starts from Longinus' view that the sublime produces a violent effect but takes it much further in maintaining that the degree of violence is a measure for the value of the emotion. He then argues that pain and terror can be more violent than pleasure, and that these emotions are, therefore, the chief sources of the sublime. "Whatever is fitted in any sort to excite pain and danger, that is to say whatever is in any sort terrible, or is conversant about terrible objects, or operates in a manner analogous to terror is a source of the Sublime; that is, it is productive of the strongest emotions which the mind is capable of feeling." As for Longinus, the passion aroused by the sublime is astonishment, but Burke defines more precisely the qualities which go to arouse it: terror, obscurity, power, vastness, infinity, difficulty, magnificence, and darkness.

Naturally this new definition of the sublime brings with it new examples. Burke is primarily concerned with literature and his examples are mainly drawn from written works. He admits very few classical authors into the category, the most important being Lucretius, for the description of the storm at the beginning of Book III, and Virgil, for the descent of Aeneas into Hades in Book VI of the *Aeneid*. The Bible is far more productive of sublime passages, though only the Old Testament. The books most favoured by Burke are Psalms and Job. Shakespeare is only quoted once, in the section on "Magnificence," for the description of the king's army in *Henry IV,* Part I.[8] Milton provides many more examples, particularly from *Paradise Lost,* in which Burke singles out as the most purely sublime passage the description of Satan, Sin, and Death at the Gates of Hell.

In the visual arts Burke quotes only one instance of the sublime, and

---

[8] Act IV, scene 1.

that, surprisingly enough, is Stonehenge, which qualifies on the grounds of its size and the difficulty of its construction.

Burke may be said to have transformed the sublime from a classical into an anti-classical conception, and to have transferred it from classical to Hebrew literature. In this he was to some extent following in the steps of Bishop Lowth, who in his lectures on Hebrew poetry, given at Oxford in the years 1741–50, emphasized the association of the sublime with the books of the Old Testament, quoting Job as the supreme example. This enthusiasm for the Old Testament, suggested by Lowth and taken up by Burke, was to become common at the time of the Romantic movement. Coleridge, for instance, writes in terms which echo Burke and Lowth: "Could you ever discover anything sublime, in our sense of the term, in the Classical Greek literature? I never could. Sublimity is Hebrew by birth." [9]

Blake does not develop a complete theory of the sublime, but he uses the word regularly as a term of the highest praise and as one describing the art of which he approves. His relation to Burke is complicated. He complains that Burke "mocks inspiration and vision," [10] but in many ways he follows his ideas on the sublime. It is a curious fact that Stonehenge, the one work of architecture picked out by Burke as sublime, should play so large a part in Blake's art (cf. Plate 48b). Admittedly it has for him a specific symbolical meaning, but the importance attached to it by Burke may have strengthened his interest in it. It is, however, above all in his passionate enthusiasm for Hebrew literature as opposed to the poetry of Greece and Rome that Blake follows Burke closely. For

[9] See also *The Letters of S. T. Coleridge,* ed. by E. T. Coleridge (London and Boston, 1895), I, 199, 405 f.; *Table Talk,* 25 July 1832 (cf. *The Table Talk and Omniana* [London, 1896], p. 174).

[10] *Works,* p. 1011. He also differed from Burke in one important detail. For Burke vagueness was one of the elements essential to the sublime, whereas for Blake all imaginative art had to be precisely defined, or, to use his own terms, "minutely articulated."

Blake true poetry (that is to say, vision) is only to be found in the Bible. The Prophets of the Old Testament were the vehicles of Divine Inspiration, and all other writers, including the poets of classical antiquity, were but faint imitators of their great Hebrew predecessors.[11]

Blake, however, went further than this and extended the argument from literature to the visual arts. In his view the masterpieces of Greek and Roman art were, like the masterpieces of classical literature, copies of Hebrew originals. The originals themselves were lost in this case, but Blake was privileged to see them in his visions:

The Artist having been taken in vision into the ancient republics, monarchies, and patriarchates of Asia has seen those wonderful originals, called in the Sacred Scriptures the Cherubim, which were sculptured and painted on walls of Temples, Towers, Cities, Palaces, and erected in the highly cultivated states of Egypt, Moab, Edom, Aram, among the Rivers of Paradise, being originals from which the Greeks and Hetrurians copied Hercules Farnese, Venus of Medicis, Apollo Belvidere, and all the grand works of ancient art. They were executed in a very superior style to those justly admired copies, being with their accompaniments terrific and grand in the highest degree. The Artist has endeavoured to emulate the grandeur of those seen in his vision, and to apply it to modern Heroes, on a smaller scale.

No man can believe that either Homer's Mythology, or Ovid's, were the production of Greece or of Latium; neither will any one believe that the Greek statues, as they are called, were the invention of Greek Artists; perhaps the Torso is the only original work remaining; all the rest are evidently copies, though fine ones, from greater works of the Asiatic Patriarchs. The Greek Muses are daughters of Mnemosyne, or Memory, and not of Inspiration or Imagination, therefore not authors of such sublime conceptions.[12]

[11] This idea was already current in the seventeenth century when Tommaso Campanella wrote in his *Poetics* (*Tutte le Opere di T. Campanella,* ed. by L. Firpo [Verona, 1954], I, 1055) that the Jews, or more precisely King David, had invented every possible literary form, and that the pagan poets discovered nothing new.

[12] *Works,* p. 780.

In so far as this theory concerns architecture Blake is here following, probably consciously, a train of thought which had been in existence since the sixteenth century. At that time certain writers argued that the true proportions for architecture were to be found in the directions given by God to Solomon for the construction of the Temple and in the description of the New Jerusalem, recorded by Ezekiel on the basis of a divinely inspired vision. This idea is hinted at by Francesco Giorgi,[13] developed by Philibert de l'Orme,[14] and given its fullest and most extended exposition by the two Jesuits Pradus and Villapandus in their commentary upon Ezekiel, published in 1596–1605. Blake almost certainly knew this work, which was much studied throughout the seventeenth and eighteenth centuries, partly because of its magnificent plates recording the authors' reconstruction of the Temple; but he could have found the theory in more convenient form in a work published in 1741 by Wood of Bath, entitled *The Origin of Building, or the Plagiarism of the Heathen Detected*.[15] The thesis of all these writers is that the principles of architecture were dictated by God to the Jews and were carried to the rest of the world by the scattering of the tribes of Israel. Fanciful though this theory may appear, it was widely upheld, but Blake seems to have been alone in extending it yet further to include sculpture. It is typical of him not to be deterred by the knowledge that the Hebrew religion forbade the representation of the human form and in spite of this to have maintained that the *Torso* and the *Apollo Belvedere* were faint echoes of the statues made by the Jewish patriarchs, just as the *Aeneid* and the *Iliad* were poor copies of the Books of Moses.[16]

---

[13] Cf. R. Wittkower, *Architectural Principles in the Age of Humanism* (London, 1949), p. 136.

[14] A. Blunt, *Philibert de l'Orme* (London, 1958), pp. 124-33.

[15] Cf. Wittkower, *Journal of the Warburg and Courtauld Institutes,* VI (1943), 220-22.

[16] Blake adds a further gloss to the accepted theory, because for him the primitive art of all nations is theoretically of equal value, the Hebrew antiquities being distinguished by the fact that, in literature at least, they have survived whereas the others are lost (cf. *Works,* p. 781).

On the art of the Patriarchs Blake's ideas were highly personal, but in his general approach towards the problem of history painting he was in close sympathy with the artists of his immediate circle, particularly in choice of subjects, many of which coincide with those recommended by Burke. From the Old Testament, for instance, Barry had selected as the theme of one of his engravings (Plate 9c), dedicated, incidentally, to Burke, a subject from the Book of Job, a work which was to occupy Blake over many years. It is, moreover, worth noticing that the latter, in his *Book of Job,* selects for the theme of one of his plates the words "Then a spirit passed before my face; the hair of my flesh stood up," a passage particularly selected by Burke as an example of the sublime.[17]

Mortimer made engravings of *Nebuchadnezzar* and *Death on the Pale Horse* (Plates 31a, 31b), both subjects extremely rare at the time but in full accord with Burke's idea of the sublime and later illustrated by Blake. From Shakespeare Blake took many subjects, but it is significant that they include one from the only passage quoted in full by Burke, namely the description of Prince Henry from *Henry IV,* Part I,[18] and a large proportion of the others illustrate the kind of horrid theme which

[17] *Ibid.,* p. 63.

[18] This is the subject of the water-colour at the end of the second folio in the British Museum with illustrations by Blake and other artists, described by T. S. R. Boase in the *British Museum Quarterly,* XX (1955), 4 ff. Boase did not identify the subject of the water-colour, which is, however, clearly identical with a composition mentioned by Blake in the *Descriptive Catalogue* of his exhibition of 1809 with the following note: "A Spirit vaulting from a cloud to turn and wind a fiery Pegasus.—Shakespeare. The Horse of Intellect is leaping from the cliffs of Memory and Reasoning; it is a barren Rock; it is also called the Barren Waste of Locke and Newton" (*Works,* p. 800). The picture actually exhibited cannot have been identical with that in the second folio, because it is described as being in the technique which Blake called "fresco" whereas the other is in water-colour, but the descriptions agree exactly, and from the fact that the water-colour is dated 1809, the year of the exhibition, it may be concluded that John Parkhurst, who commissioned the illustrations to the folio, saw the painting in the exhibition and asked Blake to make a version of it in water-colour which he could include in his extra-illustrated volume. The fact that it is bound in at the end and not in its proper place before the play which it illustrates suggests that the subject was lost sight of at an early date. This is not surprising, since Blake has used great freedom in his interpretation of the text of Shakespeare.

his contemporaries chose with particular pleasure from the tragedies and the histories: Richard III and the ghosts (Plate 11*b*), Hamlet and his father's ghost (Plate 41*c*), the ghost of Caesar appearing to Brutus, the ghost of Banquo appearing to Macbeth (Plate 12*c*), Lady Macbeth and the sleeping Duncan (Plate 13*a*), Lear and Cordelia (Plate 8*a*). All these subjects can be paralleled in drawings or paintings by Fuseli (Plate 11*c*, 13*b*, 41*a*), or Romney (Plate 13*c*), and in many cases the rendering as well as the choice of subject is closely similar to that of Blake.

Blake seems not to have interested himself seriously in the illustration of Milton till after 1800, and when he did so, it was for special and personal reasons which will be examined later. Some of his earlier designs, however, such as the *Lazar House* of 1795 (Plate 27*a*), show that he was aware of the importance of *Paradise Lost* at a relatively early period, and at that time his choice tended towards the grim themes which his friends, such as Fuseli (Plate 27*b*), preferred in the poet. In connection with Burke and his views on Milton, it is significant that Blake, Barry, Fuseli, and Stothard all made illustrations to the episode of Satan, Sin, and Death at the Gates of Hell which Burke had singled out as the purest example of the sublime (Plates 10*a*–10*c*, 11*a*). Their renderings of the subject bring out the strength and weakness of each artist: Barry literal and precise, and using an idiom derived from Michelangelo; Stothard reducing the scene to drawing-room terms; Fuseli violent in his Mannerist distortions and foreshortenings; Blake crude and yet by his very directness convincing.[19]

A number of these illustrations to Shakespeare and Milton were made at a relatively late period in Blake's career, and they underline the fact that even as a mature artist he had much in common with the painters

[19] Hogarth's illustration of the same subject, known from an engraving by Townley, is rightly recorded by Ireland (*Graphic Illustrations of Hogarth* [London, 1799], p. 578) as one of his failures, and as being possibly intended satirically.

whom he had known and admired in his youth. As will be shown later, he continued not merely to admire them but also to borrow motives from their works, even at a time when he had struck out on a line completely personal, completely new, and far beyond the ken of his more prosaically minded friends.

3. Vision and Execution in Blake's Painting

BLAKE'S THEORIES of art and of poetry were based on a whole-hearted and unqualified belief in the power of imagination and the reality of inspiration: "One power alone makes a poet: Imagination, the Divine Vision." [1] His own account of his methods of work is perfectly clear but in some ways misleading. He believed himself to be in immediate contact with "spirits" who revealed to him his visions and inspired his poems: "I am under the direction of Messengers from Heaven, Daily and Nightly," [2] he writes, and sometimes he describes their visitations in terms so immediate as to be disturbing: "The Prophets Isaiah and Ezekiel dined with me, and I asked them. . . ." [3] In the case of his written works he believed his inspiration to be of the most direct kind. Of his long epic *Milton* he writes to his friend Butts: "I have written this Poem from immediate Dictation, twelve or sometimes twenty or thirty lines at a time, without Premeditation & even against my Will"; and in another letter he says of the same poem: "I may praise it, since I dare not pretend to be any other than the Secretary; the Authors are in Eternity." [4] On the other hand, however much he was basically indebted in his poetry to dictation from an external source, he was not a slave to it and like all poets he altered and improved his first drafts. This is proved by man-

[1] *Works*, p. 1024.   [2] *Ibid.*, p. 1061.
[3] *Ibid.*, p. 195.   [4] *Ibid.*, pp. 1073, 1076.

uscripts like the Rossetti Notebook, in which different versions of a poem occur, each of them with deletions and alterations.

It it is also clear from one statement by Blake that he used the word *dictation* in a rather special sense. In the *Address* at the beginning of *Jerusalem* he writes: "When this Verse was first dictated to me, I consider'd a Monotonous Cadence, like that used by Milton & Shakespeare & all writers of English Blank Verse, derived from the modern bondage of Rhyming, to be a necessary and indispensible part of Verse. But I soon found that in the mouth of a true Orator such monotony was not only awkward, but as much a bondage as rhyme itself. I therefore have produced a variety in every line, both of cadences & number of syllables." [5] That is to say, the actual form of the composition was not dictated to the poet who was at liberty to choose his own metre; and we are forced to the conclusion that in this case it was more the ideas than the actual words which came to him from the spirits. It is, however, also probable that Blake possessed to an unusually high degree the faculty not uncommon in a poet of finding whole lines or groups of lines coming into his mind complete without any conscious effort on his part.

His ideas on art are closely similar. His purpose in life, he said, was to "See Visions, Dream Dreams & prophecy & speak Parables." [6] For him painting has nothing to do with the imitation of the material world, but is an imaginative art of the same kind as poetry: "Shall Painting be confined to the sordid drudgery of fac-simile representations of merely mortal and perishing substances, and not be as poetry and music are, elevated into its own proper sphere of invention and visionary conception? No, it shall not be so! Painting, as well as poetry and music, exists and exults in immortal thoughts." [7]

[5] *Ibid.*, p. 551.   [6] *Ibid.*, p. 1073.

[7] *Ibid.*, p. 794. Cf. also p. 816: "No Man of Sense ever supposes that copying from Nature is the Art of Painting; if Art is no more than this, it is no better than any other Manual Labour; anybody may do it and the fool often will do it best as it is a work of no Mind.",

From certain evidence, particularly from the account left by Cunningham of his making the *Visionary Heads,* one would be led to suppose that Blake suffered from actual delusions. Cunningham tells how Blake used to sit with Varley and Linnell, who would ask him to draw some historical character. A typical passage is the account of his drawing the portraits of William Wallace and Edward I:

He was requested to draw the likeness of William Wallace—the eye of Blake sparkled, for he admired heroes. "William Wallace!" he exclaimed, "I see him now, there, there, how noble he looks—reach me my things!" Having drawn for some time, with the same care of hand and steadiness of eye, as if a living sitter had been before him, Blake stopped suddenly and said, "I cannot finish him—Edward the First has stept in between him and me." "That's lucky," said his friend, "for I want the portrait of Edward too." Blake took another sheet of paper, and sketched the features of Plantagenet; upon which his Majesty politely vanished, and the artist finished the head of Wallace.[8]

There is some reason to think that in this case Blake deliberately played up to the expectations of Varley and Linnell and may have talked of these appearances as being more like real physical visions than they actually were, but on other occasions he makes his meaning plainer. The passage of which the beginning has been quoted above is significant:

The Prophets Isaiah and Ezekiel dined with me, and I asked them how they dared so roundly to assert that God spoke to them; and whether they did not think at the time that they would be misunderstood, and so be the cause of imposition.

Isaiah answer'd: "I saw no God, nor heard any, in a finite organical perception; but my senses discover'd the infinite in every thing, and as I was then

---

and p. 819: "I obstinately adhere to the true Style of Art . . . the Art of Invention, not of Imitation. Imagination is My World; this World of Dross is beneath my Notice."

[8] Cunningham's account is quoted in full by Mona Wilson (*The Life of William Blake,* pp. 256 ff.).

perswaded, and remain confirm'd, that the voice of honest indignation is the voice of God, I cared not for consequences, but wrote." [9]

Gilchrist records an amusing story which brings out the same point in more fanciful form:

At one of Mr. Ader's parties . . . Blake was talking to a little group gathered round him, within hearing of a lady whose children had just come home from boarding school for the holidays. "The other evening," said Blake, in his usual quiet way, "taking a walk, I came to a meadow and, at the farthest corner of it, I saw a fold of lambs. Coming nearer, the ground blushed with flowers; and the wattled cote and its woolly tenants were of an exquisite pastoral beauty. But I looked again, and it proved to be no living flock, but beautiful sculpture." The lady, thinking this a capital holiday show for her children, eagerly interposed: "I beg pardon, Mr. Blake, but *may* I ask *where* you saw this?" "Here, madam," answered Blake, touching his forehead.[10]

Blake, therefore, understood the exact nature of his visions, and, although he spoke of them as if they were real, he was aware that they were different from the process of seeing the material world. They were real—in fact for him they were more real than the world around him—but they were real in a special sense. His view is summed up in a passage from the *Descriptive Catalogue*:

I assert for My Self that I do not behold the outward Creation & that to me it is hindrance & not Action; it is as the dirt upon my feet, No part of Me. "What," it will be Question'd, "When the Sun rises, do you not see a round disk of fire somewhat like a Guinea?" O no, no, I see an Innumerable company of the Heavenly host crying, "Holy, Holy, Holy is the Lord God Almighty." [11]

The artist, that is to say, does not study the material world for its own sake but regards it as a series of symbols behind which lies truth; and this truth can be apprehended provided the artist has the key with

[9] *Works*, p. 195.   [10] *Ibid.*, p. 317.   [11] *Ibid.*, p. 844.

which to penetrate the mystery. The key is, of course, provided by the imagination. This faculty enables the artist, as Blake says, to see *through* not *with* the eye [12] and so to penetrate beyond the finite to the infinite and to reach direct communion with the divine: "He who sees the infinite in all things sees God; he who sees the ratio [13] only sees himself only." [14] It is this perception of the infinite that distinguishes Blake's vision from allegory or fable: "Vision or Imagination is a Representation of what Eternally Exists, Really and Unchangeably. Fable or Allegory is Form'd by the daughters of Memory. Imagination is surrounded by the daughters of Inspiration." [15] And Blake goes on to explain that allegory and fable are the mode of expression of the Greeks but that vision is the characteristic of the prophets of the Old Testament who were inspired by the Poetic or Prophetic genius, the source of all truth.[16]

The painter must, therefore, not concern himself with visible appearances but with the eternal truth lying behind them. Holding this view, Blake was naturally strongly opposed to Reynolds' views about nature. Reynolds, whose ideas were basically Aristotelian, believed that the artist could attain to ideal beauty by generalising from natural forms. To this Blake has two objections to make. First, you can never attain anything worth while if you start from nature; you must first "travel to Heaven" [17] for the vision and then seek in nature the forms with which

[12] *Ibid.*, p. 844. As Selincourt has pointed out (*William Blake*, p. 73) this idea is very close to one expressed by Plato in the *Theætetus*.

[13] I.e., that which can be perceived by reason.

[14] *Works*, p. 829.   [15] *Ibid.*, pp. 828 f.

[16] He does, however, allow that a part of real vision is to be found in the works of ancient Greek and Latin poets, but only as a faint echo of the true inspiration of the Hebrew prophets (*ibid.*, p. 831). In one context, moreover, he defines the "Most Sublime Poetry" as "Allegory addressed to the Intellectual powers, while it is altogether hidden from the Corporeal Understanding" (*ibid.*, p. 1076), but this is as part of the defence of the obscurity of his verse and is not meant in contrast to vision.

[17] *Ibid.*, p. 987. Cf. also p. 989: "All Forms are Perfect in the Poet's Mind, but these are not Abstracted nor compounded from Nature, but are from Imagination."

to express it. Second, "To Generalise is to be an Idiot," [18] because visions are always particular.

What Blake meant by this idea can be partly deduced from scattered remarks in his comments on Reynolds' *Discourses* and others in his *Descriptive Catalogue,* sometimes referring directly to painting, sometimes to poetry, but applicable equally to both. Art is not concerned with ideal beauty nor yet with moral qualities: "The Whole Bible is fill'd with Imagination and Visions from End to End and not with Moral Virtues; that is the baseness of Plato and the Greeks." [19] Art is concerned with the eternal characteristics of individuals. In speaking of Chaucer's *Canterbury Pilgrims* Blake writes: "Chaucer makes every one of his characters perfect in his kind; every one is . . . the image of a class, and not of an imperfect individual. . . . Visions of these eternal principles or characters of human life appear to poets, in all ages," [20] and these eternal principles are the substance of Blake's visions and the object of art.

But, Blake goes on, these characteristics are precise and not general and must be precisely defined. In his description of the painting of the *Last Judgement* he writes: "General Knowledge is Remote Knowledge; it is in Particulars that Wisdom consists & Happiness too. Both in Art & in Life, General Masses are as Much Art as a Pasteboard Man is Human. Every Man has Eyes, Nose & Mouth; this Every Idiot knows, but he who enters into & discriminates most minutely the Manners & Intentions, the Characters in all their branches, is the alone Wise or Sensible Man, & on this discrimination All Art is founded." [21]

[18] *Ibid.,* p. 977.
[19] *Ibid.,* p. 1022. The manuscript is difficult to decipher, and it may be correct to read *business* rather than *baseness.*
[20] *Ibid.,* pp. 787 f.
[21] *Ibid.,* pp. 836 f. In another passage from the same account (pp. 829 f.) Blake expresses the same idea in almost Platonic terms.

Each being, therefore, has its own identity or imaginative form, and this form is unchanging in eternity, though subject to apparent change in the material world. "Harmony and Proportion are Qualities & not Things. The Harmony & Proportion of a Horse are not the same with those of a Bull. Every Thing has its own Harmony & Proportion, Two Inferior Qualities in it. For its Reality is its Imaginative Form." [22] "In Eternity one Thing never Changes into another Thing. Each Identity is Eternal . . . but Eternal Identity is one thing & Corporeal Vegetation is another thing. Changing Water into Wine by Jesus & into Blood by Moses relates to Vegetable Nature also." [23]

Naturally this belief in the fundamental importance of specific characteristics brings Blake into sharp conflict with Reynolds, who held the view that too marked character was incompatible with ideal beauty. "Leanness or Fatness is not Deformity," says Blake, "but Reynolds thought Character Itself Extravagance & Deformity. Age & Youth are not Classes, but Properties of Each Class; so are Leanness & Fatness." [24] When Reynolds writes: "Peculiar marks, I hold to be, generally, if not always defects," Blake comments: "Peculiar Marks are the Only Merit"; and when on the next page Reynolds repeats the same idea in different words: "Peculiarities in the works of art, are like those in the human figure: . . . they are always so many blemishes," Blake bursts out: "Infernal Falshood!" [25] In the previous *Discourse* Reynolds had already incurred Blake's wrath by writing: "If you mean to preserve the most perfect beauty in its most perfect state, you cannot express the passions," to which Blake retaliates: "What Nonsense! Passion & Expression is Beauty Itself." [26]

It is, therefore, the primary business of the artist to express with the

[22] *Ibid.*, p. 1022.   [23] *Ibid.*, pp. 831 f. *Vegetable* is Blake's normal word for *material.*
[24] *Ibid.*, p. 990.   [25] *Ibid.*, p. 1005.   [26] *Ibid.*, p. 997.

greatest clarity the characteristics of the persons whom he depicts, and this clarity demands the highest possible degree of precision and definition. This is the basis for Blake's constantly repeated demand for sharpness of outline and minuteness of detail. "Where there are no lineaments there can be no character." [27] "Neither character nor expression can exist without firm and determinate outline . . . the more distinct, sharp, and wirey the bounding line, the more perfect the work of art, and the less keen and sharp, the greater is the evidence of weak imitation, plagiarism, and bungling. . . . How do we distinguish the oak from the beech, the horse from the ox, but by the bounding outline? . . . Leave out this line, and you leave out life itself." [28]

Blake maintained, moreover, that his visions were not, as might be supposed, vague and undefined but sharp and minutely clear. "A Spirit and a Vision are not, as the modern philosophy supposes, a cloudy vapour, or a nothing: they are organized and minutely articulated beyond all that the mortal and perishing nature can produce. He who does not imagine in stronger and better lineaments, and in stronger and better light than his perishing and mortal eyes can see, does not imagine at all. The painter of this work [29] asserts that all his imaginations appear to him infinitely more perfect and more minutely organized than anything seen by his mortal eye." [30] "Nature has no Outline, but Imagination has." [31] And since visions are of this kind, they can only be properly recorded in a work of art by "minutely Appropriate Execution." [32]

Blake demands the same clarity in colour as in outline, and it is this view that leads to his loathing, repeated on almost every page of his writings on painting, for all the schools based on colour in the modern

[27] *Ibid.*, pp. 792 f.   [28] *Ibid.*, pp. 805 f.
[29] The painting of *The Bard* from Gray.   [30] *Works*, p. 795.   [31] *Ibid.*, p. 769.
[32] *Ibid.*, p. 814. Blake's whole emphasis on the importance of outline is in essence a variation on Michelangelo's concept of *disegno*, which he would have known through Vasari.

sense, all the Venetians, Rubens, and Rembrandt. Blake's attacks on these schools are too well-known to be repeated in detail;[33] one example will give the flavour of them:

> You must agree that Rubens was a Fool,
> And yet you make him master of your School
> And give more money for his slobberings
> Than you will give for Rafael's finest Things.
> I understood Christ was a Carpenter
> And not a Brewer's Servant, my good Sir.[34]

The basis of his attack on the colourists is that the broken colour, the *sfumato* and the *chiaroscuro* of the Venetians, destroys the outline and therefore takes away what is most essential in the art of painting.[35]

For Blake, therefore, the creation of a work of art starts with a sharply defined vision which has to be recorded in the clearest possible manner. Though the vision is the starting point in this process, the execution is also essential, and it would give quite a false impression of Blake's aims and methods to over-emphasize the visionary aspect of his art and to slur over the practical.

In some cases it is possible to follow the process by which Blake arrived at his final rendering. In the case of the *Creation of Eve,* for instance the first sketch (Plate 46*a*) is a mere notation in a few rapidly drawn lines of the poses of the three figures, with no indication of anatomical detail and no hint of a setting. In a second version, in watercolour, greater precision is given to the drawing and the poses are slightly

[33] Typical examples are to be found in the *Descriptive Catalogue* (in *Works*, pp. 778 f., 802 f., 818), the epigrams (*ibid.*, pp. 851 ff.) and throughout the comments on Reynolds.
[34] *Works*, p. 851. The word *slobbering* seems to have been a common term of contempt. It is used, for instance, by John Thelwall to Coleridge and explained as meaning "the drivelling of decayed intellect." See *Letters of Coleridge* (London and Boston, 1895), I, 200 n. 2.
[35] In his attacks on the colourists Blake follows Barry very closely, even to the use of certain characteristic terms, such as the adjective *slobbering* applied to Rubens.

altered; the arm of God the Father is raised a little, giving greater solemnity to the gesture of creation; the pose of Adam indicates more posi-
tively the complete relaxation of sleep and the leaf-like form on which
he lies is more clearly defined; the crescent moon is moved, so that it
is exactly above the figure of Eve and the hand of God. In the final
composition (Plate 46b) the whole design is elaborated in detail: the
"leaf" on which Adam lies is edged with flame-like tongues and the
trees in the background are articulated with a minute, jewelled *cloisonné*
effect.

Another clear example is to be seen in the design of *Satan Smiting
Job,* which Blake repeated several times during the later years of his life.
His final statement of the composition is the tempera painting in the Tate
Gallery, executed only a short time after the engraved version for the
Illustrations of the Book of Job but fundamentally different from it.[36] In
the tempera Blake has given Satan a huge pair of bat's wings, which provide a new formal theme for the design as a whole. The cusped shape
of the wings is echoed in inverted form by the cloud behind Satan, and
again in the outer radiance of the setting sun. The result is a sharpness
and brilliance of design entirely lacking in the engraved version.

In evolving his designs, therefore, Blake makes use of the ordinary
methods employed by more conventional artists, and in yet another way
his manner of work was unexpectedly close to the academic practice of
his own time. It may seem paradoxical, but it is true to say that Blake,

[36] Before the engravings Blake made two sets of water-colours, one for Butts, one for
Linnell (see Binyon and Keynes, *Illustrations of the Book of Job*). The third set, the so-
called New Zealand set of drawings, was certainly made after the engravings and
combines elements from the latter and from the Linnell water-colours. The fact that
it contains nothing which is not to be found in one or other of these sources is a strong
argument for thinking that the set was not executed by Blake, and this view is confirmed
by the technique, which, though exquisite, is more that of Blake's followers, such as
Samuel Palmer or Calvert. I am inclined to believe that these water-colours are copies by
one or other of these artists, who would have been in a position to know both the engravings and the Linnell water-colours.

who was by far the most original English artist of his time, borrowed more extensively and more systematically from the works of other artists than did any of his contemporaries. It was, of course, a doctrine accepted since the sixteenth century that an artist should train himself by studying the works of the great masters and should incorporate in his painting motives borrowed from them, an idea which had been given its fullest expression in the *Discourses* of Sir Joshua Reynolds. Blake's method of borrowing is, however, different. Reynolds, following the academic doctrine of French and Italian art in the seventeenth century, not only wished the artist to borrow and adapt poses or themes from the strictly limited canon of accepted masters, but encouraged him to emulate the style of these masters. With Blake, however, we find that, although his chief admiration was, as we have seen, for Raphael, Michelangelo, and the artists of the Middle Ages, he was prepared to borrow ideas from a very much wider range of works, some of them relatively trivial in quality. Secondly, except in the case of the masters whom he revered, he makes no attempt to imitate the style of those from whom he pilfers ideas. When he borrows a pose from some other artist, he so completely transforms the figure that it seems to be wholly Blakean and shows at first sight no trace of its alien origin. Indeed it seems probable that Blake was often unaware that he was borrowing, and, when he was once challenged on an individual case, he denied that he had ever seen the original which he was accused of imitating. The evidence to show that he did borrow extensively is, however, overwhelming, and one is forced to conclude that Blake's visual memory was so remarkable that, if he had once seen an image, it was retained in the great storehouse of his imagination, together with thousands of other images derived from nature, or other works of art, or the invention of his own fantasy. In fact the same process seems to have taken place in his paintings as in his thought, for ideas from a hundred philosophers, theologians, and poets were absorbed into his mind and emerged, blended and altered, in the rich if tortuous web of the Prophetic Books.

The range of sources from which Blake derived visual themes is surprisingly wide, particularly for an artist of his time. He draws not only on the obvious models, such as Greek and Roman sculpture or engravings after the great masters of the sixteenth century, and on mediaeval sculpture, of which, as we have seen, he was an enthusiastic admirer, but also, more surprisingly, on works of oriental art which were beginning to be known in his day.[37]

The way in which he uses themes borrowed from other artists varies considerably. In some cases he seizes on a whole pattern and adapts it to a different use; so, for instance, he took the motive of a Gothic boss in York Minster, which he probably knew through a drawing made by Flaxman [38] (Plate 42b), and used it on a series of occasions: in the water-colour of *God Blessing the Seventh Day* (Plate 42a), in one of the illustrations to Milton's *Hymn on the Morning of Christ's Nativity* (Plate 42c), and in one of the late drawings to the Book of Enoch (Plate 42d). In other cases he seems to have studied the initials of mediaeval manuscripts, which were, as we shall see, the models on which he based his own system of illumination; and in the case of the water-colour of *St. Michael* (Plate 39a) we may even conclude that he must have known a manuscript such as the Winchester Bible, which contains one initial strikingly similar in design [39] (Plate 39b).

The celebrated colour-print *Glad Day* (Plates 1, 7a) presents a partic-

[37] For a more detailed treatment of Blake's sources, see C. H. Collins Baker, *Huntingdon Library Quarterly*, IV (1941), 359, and the present writer's article in the *Journal of the Warburg and Courtauld Institutes*, VI (1943), 190–212.

[38] Reproduced in a lithograph illustrating Flaxman's *Lectures on Sculpture*, Plate 6.

[39] There is no proof that Blake ever went to Winchester, but he might well have done so from Felpham.

ularly curious problem from the point of view of derivation. It has in such strong measure the freshness that one associates with Blake's finest works that it seems absurd at first sight to suggest that it is anything but a completely original invention, and yet, the pose is almost certainly borrowed from an existing design. I have in another context [40] called attention to the striking similarity between *Glad Day* and a small, coarse wood-engraving in Scamozzi's treatise on architecture illustrating the proportions of the human figure (Plate 7*b*). It is not at all inconceivable that Blake, with his wide reading and great curiosity, should have known this particular diagram. But there is another possible source, perhaps even more plausible. In the great series of volumes publishing the recent discoveries at Herculaneum and Pompeii, which appeared between the years 1755 and 1792, one part entitled *De' Bronzi di Ercolano* (1767–71) contains two engravings of a bronze Faun (Plates 6*a*, 6*b*) which is not only strikingly close to *Glad Day* in pose but has a lightness and delicacy totally lacking in Scamozzi's diagram. Blake must certainly have known the Herculaneum volumes, and it seems likely that the bronze stuck in his mind. This hypothesis is confirmed by a further point. One of the engravings shows the statuette from the front and the other from behind; and, curiously enough, there are two drawings by Blake on the *recto* and *verso* of a single sheet (Plates 6*c*, 7*c*), one of which is an exact study for the *Glad Day* print, and the other of which shows the same figure, but in back view. The two drawings, therefore, correspond very closely with the two engravings, the only difference being that, whereas naturally the statuette is shown standing on the same leg in both engravings, Blake draws his front view with the figure standing on the left leg and the back view with it standing on the right. The back view sketch was used by Blake for the figure of Albion in the magnificent plate illustrating the dialogue between Albion and Christ on the Cross

[40] *Journal of the Warburg Institute*, II (1938), 65 ff.

in *Jerusalem* (Plate 48*a*), designed some forty years after the drawing itself was made.[41]

As we have already seen, Michelangelo was throughout Blake's life a constant source of inspiration for him, and the motives from his work recurring in Blake's designs are legion. In one case the whole process can be traced with particular clarity. The colour-printed drawing of *Newton* (Plate 30*c*) is evidently based on Michelangelo's figure of Abias in one of the lunettes of the Sistine Chapel. Blake knew this through the engraving by Ghisi (Plate 30*a*), of which he made an exact copy, now in the British Museum (Plate 30*b*). When he came to make the *Newton*, he altered the pose but preserved, and indeed almost caricatured, that sharp definition of muscles which in Ghisi's engraving is already much more emphatic than in Michelangelo's original.

In other instances Blake does not follow a single motive but combines a series of themes taken from different sources. A striking instance of this is the design usually known as *The Ancient of Days* from *Europe* (Plate 24).[42] Here the basic idea of using the compasses as a symbol for the act of creation is derived from mediaeval manuscripts (Plate 25*a*), but the forms in which the idea is clothed are taken from a different source, again one of the famous engraved books of the later eighteenth century. In this case the artist is Pellegrino Pellegrini Tibaldi, from whom Blake derives all the elements of his figure: the wind-swept hair and beard and the left leg, which come from Tibaldi's *Neptune* (Plate 25*b*), and the down-reaching right arm, which derives directly from the plunging figure in *Christ in Glory* (Plate 25*e*), although ultimately the pose goes back to the figure of Christ in Michelangelo's *Conversion of St. Paul* in the Pauline Chapel. Blake was not alone among his con-

[41] Cf. below, pp. 81 f.

[42] For a more detailed study of this design, see the present writer's article in the *Journal of the Warburg Institute*, II (1938), 53 ff.

temporaries in making use of Tibaldi's *Neptune,* for Barry adapted the head first to the figure of Philoctetes in his painting presented to the Academy at Bologna, which he engraved, and later to that of Lear in a design which Blake certainly knew.[43]

In some instances the borrowed motive is only introduced at a very late stage in the evolution of the design. Two drawings survive for the colour-print of *Pity* (Plate 28*a*) which enable us to follow the development of the design. The essential elements are there from the beginning: the dying mother, the heavenly figure riding on the "sightless courier of the air," and the "naked new-born babe"; but in the first drawing (Plate 29*a*) they are loosely disposed in a pattern much higher in format than the final design and based on two diagonal movements. In the second drawing (Plate 29*b*) the shape approaches the final print and the design has been reduced to a more horizontal form, but without that rigid emphasis on the horizontal lines which is so characteristic of the finished composition. In the last stage two important changes take place: the dying mother takes on the form of a mediaeval recumbent tomb effigy, and a second figure is introduced at the top of the design, partly no doubt because Shakespeare refers to "Heaven's Cherubin" in the plural. What is curious is the fact that this second figure is taken almost literally from an engraving after Raphael's design of *God Appearing to Isaac* in the Vatican Loggie (Plate 32*d*). In this instance, therefore, Blake only introduces his borrowed elements at the very last stage, but he does so in a different manner in the two cases. With the mother it is to give final form to a figure which has been slowly evolved along quite different lines; with the second cherub the figure is inserted exactly as it appears in Raphael's design.

Another and slightly different example of a borrowing at the last stage in the evolution of a design is provided by the *Satan Smiting Job,*

[43] See above, p. 11.

which has already been considered in another context. The introduction of bat's wings for Satan is certainly Blake's own idea and had a special significance for him as a symbol of evil, but the idea of a winged figure surrounded by bands of different coloured clouds is one which he may well have taken from a mediaeval manuscript such as the thirteenth-century Apocalypse at Lambeth Palace, which has close affinities with his design (Plate 54c).

In all these instances we can be sure that Blake could have known, and probably did know, the particular models to which his paintings bear a similarity. In certain cases, however, the similarity is great but the possibility of Blake's knowing the work seems remote. His tempera painting of *Nelson* (Plate 46d) for example, with its naked figure poised mysteriously in a circle of figures entwined in the windings of Leviathan is curiously like Pontormo's *Christ in Glory*, painted in the choir of San Lorenzo, Florence. The original fresco was destroyed in 1742 and was not engraved; the drawing for it in the Uffizi (Plate 43a) can hardly have been known to Blake; and one is forced to assume either that the resemblance is accidental or that Blake knew a copy of the painting or of the drawing. This is not inconceivable, because Pontormo was an artist much admired by Blake's friends, such as Fuseli and Flaxman, who visited Italy, and they may have made or acquired copies after his designs; but no such copy is known.

An even more curious case arises in connection with Salviati. Blake's water-colour of *Jacob's Dream* (Plate 44), with its fantastic spiral staircase up and down which angels walk—a complete novelty in the iconography of this subject—reminds one closely of Salviati's fresco of *David and Nathan* in the Palazzo Sacchetti (Plate 43b); and further, one of the plates, entitled "My Son, my Son," in the *Gates of Paradise* (Plate 43c), shows in the foreground a figure in strong contrapposto about to hurl a spear which is strangely close in movement and pose to Salviati's

Saul about to hurl his spear at David in another fresco in the same room of the Palazzo Sacchetti (Plate 43*d*). Here again we are faced with the awkward fact that this particular fresco cycle of Salviati was not engraved and seems to have been little studied in the late eighteenth century, but it is not inconceivable that Blake should have known of it through copies made by one of his friends.

The examples of Blake's borrowings so far considered all come from relatively obvious sources, but there are instances, particularly in the illustrations to *Jerusalem,* which prove that his curiosity led him further afield. The plate usually called the *Chariot of Inspiration,* which may in fact be a Time Chariot (Plate 50*b*), shows human-headed bulls certainly based on engravings after the sculptures of Persepolis from *Ouseley's Travels* (Plate 50*a*), published in 1821, from which Blake also derived other motives; the design of *Beulah Enthroned on a Sun-Flower* (Plate 50*d*), at the head of chapter III of *Jerusalem,* seems to be taken from Moor's *Hindu Pantheon* (Plate 50*c*), a work which is mentioned by Flaxman and must certainly have been known to Blake; and the figure of Pitt in the tempera painting of *Pitt Guiding Behemoth* (Plate 46*c*) is clothed in a robe clearly Oriental in character and stands against a halo of purely Buddhist type. That the resemblance is not accidental is clear from Blake's description of his two tempera paintings: "The two pictures of Nelson and Pitt are compositions of a mythological cast, similar to those Apotheoses of Persian, Hindoo, and Egyptian Antiquity, which are still preserved on rude monuments." [44]

The problem of Blake's borrowings becomes much more complex when we come to consider his relation to his contemporaries. Because Blake was a more original artist than his friends it is tempting to assume that, when a similarity exists between his works and theirs, Blake is the inventor of the idea and his friends the plagiarisers; and this idea is

[44] Cf. *Works,* p. 780.

supported by Fuseli's well-known remark, "Blake is damned good to steal from." But the evidence of the works themselves by no means shows that the traffic was one way, from Blake to his friends; on the contrary, in most of the cases in which the relative dates can be established, priority is on the side of the other artist concerned. Blake, in short, seems to have used the works of his contemporaries as freely as he did those of the dead—and in the same way, because what he took from them he made wholly his own.

We have already seen how closely Blake followed Barry and sometimes Mortimer in the early works, and to these two artists should be added a third, Stothard, whose types recur in several of Blake's engraved designs from the 1780s and even the 1790s. The figure of a girl to be found in Stothard's illustrations, for instance in one to *Ossian* (1779; Plate 12*b*),[45] is the origin of Blake's principal figure in the plate to Commins' *Elegy* of 1782 (Plate 12*a*), and reappears surprisingly in the much more personal designs for the *Book of Thel* of 1789 (Plate 20*a*). Two years later, when Blake was commissioned to illustrate the stories of Mary Wollstonecraft, he based his style on Stothard's plates to the *Unnatural Mother* (1782).[46] This was for Blake an unusual commission and it is easy to imagine why he should have felt the need to rely on the manner of another designer, but it is more curious to find that even in the *Songs of Innocence,* and in one of the most original illustrations to them, *The Shepherd* (Plate 17*a*), he seems once again to have looked at Stothard, this time at his engravings to Marmontel's *Adelaide* (1781; Plate 17*b*),[47] though the most cursory glance will show how completely he has transformed what he took.

In feeling Blake is far closer to Fuseli and Flaxman than to Stothard, and he has more themes in common with them. In certain cases there can be no doubt that Blake was the borrower and not the inventor of

[45] Cf. Coxhead, *Thomas Stothard*, p. 167.   [46] *Ibid.*, p. 46.   [47] *Ibid.*, p. 64.

these common ideas. The repeated pointing gesture of the comforters in the tenth plate to *Job* (Plate 51*a*), for instance, is remarkably like the *Three Witches* of Fuseli, painted some thirty years earlier (cf. Plate 51*b*). Here it is possible that both artists had in mind a common source, an engraving by Enea Vico after Perino del Vaga's *Fall of the Giants* in the Palazzo Doria at Genoa (Plate 51*d*), but this is not close enough to Blake's design to account for it without assuming the intervention of Fuseli's composition.[48] A striking affinity is also to be seen between Blake's water-colours of *Pestilence* and *David and Goliath* (Plates 40*a*, 40*b*), both of which date from well after 1800, and two drawings by Fuseli, *Achilles at the Pyre of Patroclus* (Plate 40*c*) and *Hamlet and the Ghost of his Father* (Plate 41*a*), which are substantially earlier. Blake has transformed the armour of the ghost into something far more bestial and has made the gesture of the striding Achilles more powerful, but in both cases the debt to Fuseli is evident.

Even in such mature works as the Dante water-colours traces of borrowing from contemporaries are perceptible. Blake's interest in Dante, which does not seem to have developed until his last years, was probably stimulated either by Fuseli, who had made drawings of Dantesque subjects in Rome in the 1770s, or by Flaxman, who had produced his Dante cycle in 1793. In one case at least, *Caiaphas and the Hypocrites* (Plate 61*a*), Blake seems to have made direct use of Flaxman's design (Plate 61*b*), though he enlarged its scope and increased its effectiveness by the addition of the landscape, the lines of which echo the poses of the hooded figures around the crucified Caiaphas.

In these cases the question of priority is clearly settled, but in others it is more doubtful. The pose of Eve in Blake's *Body of Abel Found by Adam and Eve* (Plate 57*c*), with the head thrown right forward and the hair streaming down from it, is also to be seen in a drawing by Fuseli

[48] The pose occurs again on page 93 of *Jerusalem* (Plate 51*c*).

of an unidentified subject at Zurich (Plate 57*a*). In this case neither work can be securely dated, though Blake's version must certainly be placed late in his career. Moreover, this particular mannerism, almost Parmigianesque in character, is much more in conformity with the style of Fuseli than with that of Blake, and the probability is that he was the inventor of the motive. It is also significant that it occurs, slightly modified, in another drawing by Fuseli, representing Romeo and Juliet in the balcony scene (Plate 57*b*).

Fundamentally, however, it is futile to argue the question of priority. The essential point is that there were certain motives and certain images which were, one might almost say, the common property of the whole group to which Blake, Fuseli, Flaxman, Romney, and Stothard belonged, and that each member of the group produced his own particular interpretation of the motive. This fact is well illustrated by the history of the figure of an old, bearded man with arms outstretched, which is to be found in the works of all these artists but is most familiar from Blake's *Lazar House* of 1795 (Plate 27*a*). The figure seems to appear first in this particular circle in the engraving by Blake after Fuseli which illustrates Erasmus Darwin's *Botanic Garden,* published in 1791. Here it represents the Nile, and it is natural enough to find that the artist has based the figure on a relief of Jupiter Pluvius from Montfaucon (Plate 25*c*). In Fuseli's original drawing (Plate 21*a*) the figure is loosely indicated, and in the engraving Blake has given it a sharper form much closer to Montfaucon (cf. Plate 21*b*). He then uses it himself for the *Lazar House,* a theme which Fuseli also illustrated (Plate 27*b*), though whether before or after Blake is not clear, and in any case his bat-winged figure is somewhat different, though ultimately deriving from the same source. In the meantime Flaxman had used it for his engraving of the *Statue of Four Metals* in the Dante series (Plate 25*d*), following Montfaucon fairly closely. Finally it reappears in one of Romney's most original wash-drawings (Plate 21c), which probably illustrates the lines from *Paradise Lost:*

> Thou from the first
> Wast present, and, with mighty wings outspread
> Dove-like sat'st brooding on the vast Abyss.[49]

Never did Romney come so close as in this drawing to the spirit of Blake, who, it should be added, liked him as a man and admired his imaginative designs, if not his portraiture.[50]

Another instance of various artists of this group using a common image is provided by Blake's *Good and Evil Angels Struggling for a Child,* of which four versions are known: one, probably dating from the late 1780s, was formerly in the collection of Mrs. Nöttidge (Plate 32a); a second, slightly later, belongs to Mrs. Payne Whitney; a third is on page 4 of the *Marriage of Heaven and Hell;* and the fourth is a colour-printed drawing, dated 1795, in the Tate Gallery (Plate 31c). All these are reminiscent in pattern of a wash-drawing by Flaxman in the Fitzwilliam Museum (Plate 32c), which probably dates from 1783; it represents three women, one naked and two draped, floating in front of what appears to be an arch or the entrance to a cave. A similar group was used by Fuseli for *Satan Starting at the Touch of Ithuriel's Spear,* known from a drawing and a line engraving of 1807. In Blake's hands the group becomes more and more characteristic of his style as he develops it. In the first version the chained figure is handsome in a conventional way, like the figures in Flaxman's drawing, and he gazes before him with wide-open eyes. In the later versions he becomes increasingly sinister in expression, and his eyes take on a frightening blankness which clearly indicates that he is blind, a symbol of his fallen and imperfect state.

[49] Book I, lines 19 ff.
[50] For a discussion of Romney's drawings see Crookshank, *Burlington Magazine,* XCIX (1957), 42 ff.

The analysis of Blake's relationship to his contemporaries and to the art of the past provides a curious paradox which is perhaps typical of the Romantic period (another striking case is the poetry of Coleridge): what appears to be a startlingly original and independent style is in fact built up on material derived from a wide range of sources, European and Oriental. Just as Blake's thought was enriched by his reading of the neo-Platonists, of the Christian mystics of all ages, whether orthodox or heretical, and of Oriental writers on religion, so his art was broadened and deepened by his study of everything that had gone before him —everything, that is to say, that could be relevant to his aims, for he never wasted his time in studying naturalistic painting, like that of the Dutch in the seventeenth century or the Rococo of his own day, since he knew that from them he could learn nothing. With that strange consistency, which is so typical of him, he turned to just those sources with which he felt really in sympathy: mediaeval art, the painting of Raphael and Michelangelo and their followers, and certain types of Oriental art in so far as it could be known to him. Here he found himself in contact with men who sought the spiritual values in which he believed and who were opposed to the rationalism and materialism against which he had set his face.

4. The First Illuminated Books

DURING THE YEARS 1789 to 1798 Blake's creative energies as a visual artist found expression in a new medium, engraving, which he had hitherto used almost entirely for reproducing the works of other artists, and in a new field, the illustration of his own works.[1] The first year of the period, 1789, is marked by the production of the *Songs of Innocence* (Plates 14a–19b) and the *Book of Thel* (Plate 20a), in which Blake launched on the world in complete and mature form his new method of illuminated printing.

It is true that he had made two preliminary experiments in the technique in pamphlets entitled *There Is no Natural Religion* and *All Religions Are One,* both probably engraved in 1788,[2] but these are little more than variants of the type of Emblem book familiar since the sixteenth century and popularised in England by the often reprinted volume of Quarles.

In the *Songs* and *Thel* Blake creates something entirely new and personal in the way of book production. There was, of course, nothing basically novel in attempting to combine text and illustration in a single

---

[1] During these years he produced no water-colours of importance, and the magnificent series of designs made in 1795, though in a mixed medium, are fundamentally variants of a type of engraving.

[2] The exact dates of these booklets are not known. They must have been engraved before the much more competently executed *Songs* but after 1787, for Blake said that his method of relief-engraving was revealed to him by his dead brother, Robert, who appeared to him in a dream. Blake's statements of this kind may sometimes have been fanciful, but in this case it must imply that the idea came to him after his brother's death, which took place in 1787.

finely designed page, since this had been one of the aims sought by printers since the invention of the art, though it would probably be hard to find examples in which both text and illustration were the product of a single mind. Blake's actual method of achieving his effect, however, is fundamentally original in that he fused colour and line more completely than ever before and produced something of the brilliance of the painted pages in a mediaeval manuscript. In fact his method can be defined as an attempt to recapture the effect of a mediaeval page, but in a technique which admits of reproduction.

The technique that he invented for this purpose was so curious that it needs detailed description.[3] Blake first took an ordinary copper etching-plate. On this he drew the outlines of his decorative design in a varnish resistant to acid. The effect of this was that, when the plate was immersed in the acid, the unprotected parts were bitten away, leaving the parts painted out in varnish in relief. This is roughly an inverted form of the ordinary process of etching, or a transference of the process of wood-engraving to a copper plate. It has the advantage over etching that the plate can be printed without the high pressure of a proper etching press, but it involves great technical difficulties because normally, with deep biting, the acid tends to undercut the ridge of copper protected by the varnish, and with Blake's process, where thin lines are left in relief, they could be almost entirely destroyed by this process. If, however, nitric acid is used instead of the usual sulphuric, it tends to bite more or less vertically and the undercutting is avoided.

With the text a further difficulty occurs. If it were painted in with varnish, like the designs, it would have to be done backwards. Blake's solution seems to have been to write the text in varnish on a piece of

[3] The exact method was not known till S. W. Hayter, Joan Miró, and Ruthven Todd made a series of experiments which led to their being able to repeat exactly the effects produced by Blake. These experiments are recorded by Hayter in *New Ways of Gravure* (London, 1949), pp. 85 ff., and by Todd in *Print Collector's Quarterly*, XXIX (1948), 25 ff.

paper which had previously been covered with gum-arabic. The copper plate was then heated and laid on the paper, and the writing transferred under pressure. The paper was then removed and the writing was found to be clearly imprinted in reverse in varnish on the plate, so that the text could be bitten in exactly the same way as the decoration.[4]

Once the plate was bitten, the inking remained a considerable problem. If the ink was applied with an ordinary gelatine roller, it inevitably sank into the greater part of the area which should have remained clean, so that the result of printing in this way would have been a text written in black, surrounded by a thin white line, with the rest of the field black. This effect can be avoided by inking an unengraved plate and then transferring the ink from this plate under not very high pressure to the raised surface of the engraved plate. This not only keeps the whites clean, but produces that mottled effect which is so characteristic of the pages in the printed books.[5]

This printing was usually done in a single colour—black, bluish green, or golden brown—though on very rare occasions Blake varied the colour from one part of the plate to the other, an effect which was made possible by his peculiar process of inking. The pull was then finished off in water-colours, with the result that, though in the printed outline all copies of a particular plate are more or less identical, each acquires an individual character from the colouring. Further, since Blake kept the plates of his books and often printed and coloured copies many years after he had originally engraved the plates, different copies can vary to a very striking degree. In the case of the *Songs of Innocence,* for instance, the early

[4] In fact no doubt, the text was transferred first, as the pressure of transfer might otherwise have disturbed the decorative parts.

[5] Only a fragment of one of Blake's original plates survives (in the Lessing Rosenwald Collection), but it shows that he took great pains to burnish the part of the plate bitten away by the acid, which is in fact as smooth and as even as a clean etching-plate. This process would reduce the chance of ink catching on a ridge in the bitten areas.

copies are simply coloured in rather light tones, a single wash sufficing for any one figure of decorative element,[6] whereas later versions are often treated in the richer and deeper colours which Blake preferred in his last years and are worked up in small touches, a technique which he never used in his early days.

The plates in the *Songs of Innocence* vary considerably in character and in quality, an argument in favour of the view that the engraving of the whole book probably took a considerable time and may well have been started before 1789, the date on the title page. In some pages the figure composition is conceived as a unit separate from the text and occupies the top or bottom of the page. These plates are probably the earliest to be engraved. They are close in general pattern to Blake's Emblem books of 1788; the figures are more conventional in style, and they include many which differ little from those to be found in the illustrations of a contemporary artist such as Stothard. Additional support for this view is provided by the fact that they include three poems which appear in Blake's satire *An Island in the Moon,* which was probably written about 1787.[7] Even in these more conventional plates, however, there are details which are truly Blakean. The figures in the second plate of the *Ecchoing Green* (Plate 19*a*), for instance, are depicted in contemporary dress, but they have an ethereal quality and a long swinging movement which is unlike any of Blake's contemporaries; in the *Laughing Song* the idiom is more neoclassical, but the movement is equally personal; and the frieze-like train of children in *Holy Thursday* (Plate 19*b*) has a naïve rigidity which no one else at Blake's time would

---

[6] In the Rosenwald copy of the *Blossom* Blake used a single tone of green, almost exactly like that to be found in certain early French manuscripts (e.g. the Lectionary of St. Martial of the tenth century in the Bibliothèque Nationale, MS Lat. 5901).

[7] *The Little Boy Lost, Nurse's Song,* and *Holy Thursday.* A fourth, *Laughing Song,* illustrated in the same style, is first found written on the fly-leaf of the *Poetical Sketches* and is, therefore, also probably early.

have risked. And in all these plates we see the delicate, curvilinear forms of flowers, leaves, or vine tendrils which were to be so typical of Blake's best illumination.

In a second group of plates the fusion of text and decoration is more complete. *The Shepherd* (Plate 17*a*) reminds one in many ways of Stothard, particularly of his engravings to Marmontel (Plate 17*b*), but the fantastic forms of the trees and the wanton repetition in the silhouettes of the sheep are typical of Blake; and here the scene painted in the lower half of the page strays up to the top and begins to enclose the text of the poem. In certain other cases the unity is achieved in a different manner. In the plate of the *Introduction,* "Piping down the valleys wild" (Plate 16*a*), the text is enclosed in a border composed of branches interwoven to form a series of oval panels, a device clearly taken from certain types of mediaeval manuscripts in which a series of scenes are enclosed in panels knit together by an interlacing design (Plate 16*b*).[8]

The perfect fusion of text and decoration is to be seen in three plates which must be the last of the book in time of engraving: *The Blossom* (Plate 18*a*), *Infant Joy* (Plate 15*a*), and *The Divine Image* (Plate 18*b*). Here the flame-like forms of the plants and flowers envelop the text completely and carry on the spirit of the poem so perfectly that it is impossible to separate the forms of the decoration from the ideas of the lyric. Here at least Blake has created a type of illuminated page for which no parallel can be found except in the finest manuscripts of the later Middle Ages.

Equally accomplished in its complete unity, though in a somewhat different idiom, is the title page of the *Songs* (Plate 14*a*), which shows a mother teaching two children to read, seated under a tree, the branches of which are entwined round the words of the title. What is novel here

[8] The closest parallel is to be found in a Tree of Jesse in a thirteenth-century English manuscript in Sir John Soane's Museum (Plate 16*b*).

is the form of script used for the word *Songs,* the letters of which turn into leaf-forms or support tiny figures, in a manner which was to be widely employed in the nineteenth century but which was certainly rare, and probably unique, at the time of the publication of the *Songs.*[9]

The *Book of Thel* (Plate 20*a*) represents the same stage in the evolution of Blake's art as an illustrator. The figure of Thel herself is still a Stothard type, and, except in one case, text and illustrations are fairly sharply separated from each other. The one exception is the title page, on which the words of the title, burgeoning into leaves and flowers like those of the *Songs,* are surrounded by a tree, almost Chinese in its delicacy, while the lower part of the page is filled with flowers like those of *Infant Joy,* out of which spring tiny, fairy-like figures.

The ethereal lightness and flowing beauty of the forms used in the illuminations to *Thel* and the *Songs of Innocence* are the direct reflection of the tone of the poems and of Blake's state of mind at this stage in his career. Throughout his life his philosophy was based on a variant of the belief, common among mystics, that before his birth man exists in a perfect and infinite existence, and that his arrival into this world is a kind of fall from the infinite to the finite. In youth, however, memories of his previous state remain with man, till they are gradually crushed by education and the imposition of rules and conventions. At the time of the *Songs of Innocence* Blake was still conscious of his direct contact with the infinite and living the imaginative life in its full and almost undisturbed peace. His material life was not without its difficulties, and he was not unaware of the political and social problems which existed in the world;[10] but he had not yet been embittered by them, and his faith in a solution to them was still unimpaired. In *Thel* the problem

[9] It was frequently used by Romantic illustrators, such as Grandville and Doré, and later by Kate Greenaway and the draughtsmen of *Punch.*

[10] David Erdman has shown in his *Blake: Prophet against Empire* that there is more political awareness in Blake's early works than is generally supposed.

of the fall from the infinite to the finite is the principal theme, and the hesitancy of the soul to enter into the material world is described with a certain melancholy; but the emphasis is still on the possibilities of contact with the infinite rather than on the limitations of the finite, and the tone is one of relative optimism. It is, therefore, natural that in this happy early stage of his career Blake should use for the decoration of his poems the undulating forms of flames or plants and colours which, though simple, are fresh and gay.

This happy phase did not last, and with the beginning of the French Revolution Blake's thought takes on a more serious tone. In its initial stages, however, the Revolution was for Blake a symbol of liberation from the old order. It stood for the destruction of tyranny and superstition, and Blake was among those who devoutly prayed that a similar movement of freedom might visit England.

The degree to which he was personally acquainted with the leading radicals of his day, such as Godwin, Holcroft, and Paine, has been exaggerated,[11] but there is no question that he sympathised with their ideas, since these are reflected in the two works which follow the *Songs of Innocence* and *Thel: The French Revolution* and the *Marriage of Heaven and Hell*. The first of these does not directly concern us here, since it was the one work which Blake planned to print and publish in the ordinary way, through the well-known radical bookseller Joseph Johnson, and not by his method of illuminated engraving;[12] but it is of importance in setting forth the story of the first years of the French Revolution in a manner which shows clearly that Blake was at this date a convinced Jacobin. The *Marriage of Heaven and Hell* was engraved by Blake's normal process, and though it is not one of the most successful examples of his illumination, it contains his most moving and fervent declara-

[11] It has been more exactly defined by Mr. Erdman (*ibid.,* pp. 139–47).
[12] In fact it never appeared and is known only from a proof copy.

tion of revolutionary faith. Nowhere did he state with such poetic enthusiasm his faith in energy as a means of bursting through the bonds
of convention, false morality, and reason—already for him a negative
faculty and the antithesis of imagination—and so enabling man to re-
establish contact with the world of eternity and infinity which is his
natural lot, but from which he is cut off by the limitations of the material universe. A few of the *Proverbs of Hell* in the *Marriage* are enough
to give the flavour of the whole work:

> The road of excess leads to the palace of wisdom.
> He who desires but acts not breeds pestilence.
> Prisons are built with stones of Law, Brothels with bricks of Religion.
> The cistern contains: the fountain overflows.
> The tygers of wrath are wiser than the horses of instruction.
> As the caterpillar chooses the fairest leaves to lay her eggs on, so the
>   priest lays his curse on the fairest joys.
> Exuberance is Beauty.
> Enough! or Too much.

The spirit of these violent sayings comes out in the contrast between the
two illustrations at the beginning and end of the last section of the book.
The first shows the figure of a naked youth from which emanate rays
of light, the symbol of man in his free and imaginative state; the second
shows a crude and almost grotesque figure of Nebuchadnezzar in his
madness, the image of man in his lowest state of degradation, when he
has allowed his imagination to be killed by materialism and rationalism.
Blake was later to take up this figure again and to make of it one of
his most striking designs.

   That revolutionary energy which is the central theme of the *Marriage*
infuses life into the title page of the book (Plate 22*a*). The forms are
still curvilinear, as in the decoration of the *Songs of Innocence* and *Thel,*
but they now sweep across the page with a violence which is in marked

contrast to the gaiety and lightness of the earlier decorations. The tone is more sombre than before, but the title page still expresses a conviction that energy will win the day and that man will become free.[13]

The themes treated in the *Marriage of Heaven and Hell* are taken up and expanded in three works produced in 1793. The *Visions of the Daughters of Albion* is a protest against the frustrations caused by conventional rules of sexual morality and an attack on the institution of marriage itself on the grounds that sexual relations should be based on emotion and impulse and not bound by rules. The *Gates of Paradise* embodies the same protest in the form of emblems, and adds certain doctrines which were later to become of great importance in Blake's thought: the idea that mutual forgiveness of sins is the only source of true happiness; and the contrast between Christ's doctrine of love in the New Testament and the restrictive law of Moses in the Old. *America* deals with the first stage of the revolutionary movement in which Blake had believed so passionately, but was written at the moment when he was beginning to be disillusioned with its second phase. It differs, however, from the *French Revolution* in that it is no longer a straight narrative of events but is written partly in terms of the allegorical figures which Blake was beginning to evolve, so that Washington and Tom Paine appear in alternation with Urthona and Orc.

The little emblem-cuts of the *Gates of Paradise* are of no great moment, but the *Visions* and *America* mark the transition between the

[13] There is some doubt about the exact date of the *Marriage*. In one copy page 3 is dated 1790, and in others internal evidence points to this date; but some authorities have been inclined to take it as the beginning rather than the end of the composition (see Keynes, *Blake's Illuminated Books,* p. 35) and to maintain that it was mainly written at a date nearer 1793. For myself I find this hard to believe. By that time Blake's faith in the French Revolution was greatly shaken, and in the three books printed in that year his interests seem to be quite different. At most I should be prepared to believe that the *Marriage* might have been completed in 1791, about the same time as *The French Revolution,* which is in a sense its counterpart, setting forth the actual events of a revolution which, Blake still hoped, would turn into reality the principles outlined in the *Marriage.*

energy of the *Marriage* and the gloom of the later Lambeth books. The title page and the first plate of the *Visions* (Plates 20*b*, 22*b*) have the vitality of the *Marriage,* and even something of the lightness of *Thel,* but the tone soon changes to the grimness of the crouching figures on Plate 7, or the horror of the page representing Oothon and Bromion chained back to back while Theotormon crouches in despair behind them, a group which symbolises primarily the frustrating effects of the marriage tie. In *America* the tone is gloomier. One plate shows at the top an eagle about to devour the corpse of a woman and at the bottom the body of a drowned man being eaten by fishes. This atmosphere is relieved only by the occasional appearance of the naked youth who figures in the *Marriage of Heaven and Hell,* and by the delicate page on which two children lie asleep beside a huge woolly ram under one of those weeping Chinese trees which Blake had already used in the title page of *Thel.*

The most beautiful visual expression of this stage in Blake's development is to be found in the *Songs of Experience,* finished in 1794 but probably written and even engraved during the two or three previous years. In many cases the themes provide exact parallels with those of the *Songs of Innocence,* but in a different and more sombre mood—the *Tyger* instead of the *Lamb,* the *Sick Rose* instead of the *Blossom, Infant Sorrow* instead of *Infant Joy*—and the same is true of the illustrations. The title page of *Experience* (Plate 14*b*) sums up the later mood as completely as that of *Innocence* typifies the earlier. Two dead bodies, an aged man and a woman, laid out on a bier, form the central motive, while two younger mourning figures move round them. The gay, curved forms of *Innocence* are replaced by severe horizontals in the dead figures, which are laid out like the effigies on a Gothic tomb, and the lower half of the page is completed by the simple rectilinear pattern of the architectural background. Even the script chosen for the words of the title reflects the change of tone: unadorned Roman capitals, as opposed to the fantastic vegetable-curls of the earlier letters. The contrast between the decoration of *The Sick Rose* (Plate 15*b*) and *Infant Joy* (Plate 15*a*) is equally telling. Plant-forms are still used, but now they are the angular and almost clumsy lines of a rose branch armed with grotesquely large thorns, arranged like the teeth of a saw. The rotting rose itself is as different as can be imagined from the life-giving flower in *Infant Joy*. Even when Blake repeats a device used in the earlier book it takes on a quite different character. The *Schoolboy,* for instance, has in its right margin the interlacing design which Blake had used for the *Introduction* to *Innocence,* but, instead of flowing smoothly up the page, the branches are now jagged and interrupted, producing an effect as abrupt and staccato as the other was smooth and legato. If the greatest achievements of the earlier volume are to be found in the illustrations to the happiest poems, in the later the most moving are either those to savagely bitter poems like the *Poison Tree* or the solemn night of the *Introduction*. The "Contrary States of the Human Soul" are given as clear and complete expression in the decorative treatment of the pages as they are in the text of the poems.

The years 1793 and 1794 mark a crisis for Blake and the group of radicals with whom he was associated. The September Massacres in 1792, and the execution of the King and Queen in 1793, followed by the Terror, made those whose support for the Revolution was combined with humanitarianism gradually change their views. Further, the reaction of Pitt's government to the new development in France led to a violent repression of all radicalism in England and the disruption of the group. Some, like Paine, fled to France; others were brought to trial, and though Holcroft escaped conviction, many of his friends were less fortunate and were condemned to deportation.

The intellectual members of the group found various solutions to the disillusionment which they felt at the failure of the hopes they had placed in the Revolution and the breaking up of their movement. Mary Wollstonecraft devoted herself to propaganda against social evils and the battle for the rights of women, and Godwin spent the rest of his life in pure speculation and the creation of anarchist Utopias.

Blake's solution was in many ways similar to Godwin's. He foreswore political activity and turned inwards towards "mental strife," seeking a philosophical and religious solution to the problems of the universe rather than aiming at the immediate improvement of man's state on earth. He gave his most moving expression to this recantation of his belief in revolutionary activity in *The Grey Monk,* written some years later:

> But vain the Sword and vain the Bow,
> They never can work War's overthrow.
> The Hermit's Prayer and the Widow's tear
> Alone can free the World from fear.
>
> For a Tear is an Intellectual Thing,
> And a Sigh is the Sword of an Angel King,
> And the bitter groan of the Martyr's woe
> Is an Arrow from the Almightie's Bow.

But this solution was not to be found all in a moment, and for the next five or six years Blake was to be plunged into a despair from which he only slowly emerged after 1800, as he gradually discovered a final, mystical solution to his problems.

The poems which he produced during these years, called the Lambeth Books from his new place of residence, are the darkest and gloomiest in the whole range of his work, both in their text and their illustration. Blake's bitter awareness of the evil of the world led him to a dualist belief which insisted on the existence of an original force of evil, which he called Urizen (from the Greek ὁρίζω, "to fix a limit") and identified with the Jehovah of the Old Testament in opposition to the Jesus of the New Testament, whom he identified with the force of good. This basic opposition he extended by adding to Urizen-Jehovah the attributes of reason, restraint, and law, as opposed to imagination, freedom, and love for one's neighbour, which he associated with Christ. The theme of the Lambeth Books is the struggle between reason and imagination, and in this phase of his career Blake tends to take a pessimistic view of the outcome of the struggle and prefers to paint the horrors of man's state when in the control of rationalism and materialism rather than dwell on the possibilities of recovering his freedom through the proper exercise of the imagination.

In form the Lambeth Books differ from Blake's earlier illuminated works in that the illustrations play a greater part. On the pages which contain the text of the poems the proportion of decoration is on the whole greater than previously, and each book contains a number of plates which have no text at all. In fact one could say that, whereas the earlier books consist of text with decoration added to it, now the designs play as much part as the text in the expression of Blake's ideas, and some of the full-page plates embody ideas which are not completely worked out in the poems themselves. It would also, in my opinion, be true to say that, although the Lambeth Books contain some of Blake's least successful plates, the finest of them, such as the *Ancient of Days* from *Europe* (Plate 24*a*), or certain pages from *Urizen,* represent his art at its most splendid, and are far nobler expressions of his ideas than the turgid and repetitive poems.

The earliest of these works is probably *Europe.* It contains two plates, *Plague* (Plate 23*b*) and *Famine,* which are unique among the illustrations to Blake's Prophetic Books in that the artist has chosen to depict his subject in contemporary dress and setting, almost as if he had been illustrating Mary Wollstonecraft's stories. But, generally speaking, the plates to the Lambeth Books are sombre and allusive like the poems themselves. The serpent of materialism, which had appeared in smaller form in the *Marriage of Heaven and Hell*, sprawls menacingly across the title page to *Europe*. In one plate of *Urizen* we see the evil deity sunk in the waters of materialism (Plate 23*a*), while on another Los, his antagonist and the embodiment of the Poetic Genius, howls amid the flames in which Urizen has imprisoned him. A third plate shows the embryo created by Urizen as a skeleton curled up as if in the womb, and the impression of horror is carried on through every page of the book. Some are really terrifying; some are grotesque; and some are on the very brink of the comic through their exaggeration; but all carry a certain conviction, and the best are deeply moving.

The other three Lambeth Books, the *Song of Los,* the *Book of Los,* and the *Book of Ahania,* all engraved in 1795, add little to what Blake had achieved in the illuminations to *Europe* and *Urizen,* and the most splendid plate of these years is the frontispiece to *Europe,* the *Ancient of Days* (Plate 24*a*), which we have already considered from a different point of view. It remains one of Blake's most impressive statements of what was for him at this time the central theme: the view of the creation as an evil act, and of the creator, Jehovah-Urizen, as the principle of evil, compelling man to live the bounded and restrained life of reason as opposed to the free life of the imagination. The compasses, which the colossal figure holds down onto the black emptiness below him, symbolise for Blake not the imposition of order on chaos, but the reduction of the infinite to the finite.

The ideas expressed in the frontispiece to *Europe* were expanded by Blake in a series of designs executed in 1795, which were bought ten years later by Blake's friend and patron, Thomas Butts, and of which the most important are now in the Tate Gallery. These designs, which are on a larger scale than Blake's works of the early 1790s, were executed in a special medium invented by the artist which bears some relation to his method of book illumination but is basically a variant of monotype. They were produced as follows. Blake would draw the outline in black on a piece of millboard, probably adding a certain amount of internal modelling and other details but all in one colour. This he would print off under quite low pressure on a piece of paper. Then he would colour the whole of his millboard to complete the design and again print this on top of the black outline already made. The result produced a mottled effect like that of some of the printed books, but far richer. The resulting design was touched up in water-colour, though this plays a far smaller part than it does in the printed books. It is usually stated on the authority of Tatham that these prints were made in oil colours, but, given Blake's well-known hatred of oil paint, this is intrinsically improbable, and experiment has shown that the effects can be produced with egg tempera.

There are good reasons for supposing that these colour-prints were planned by Blake as a single series. They were all produced in a very short period of time, and they are more or less identical in format and technique. Moreover, all the subjects can be shown to bear on themes connected with Blake's interpretation of the early history of the world as it is set forth in the Lambeth Books. The first in the series is the print of *God Creating Adam* (Plate 24*b*).[14] This is Blake's version of the creation of man as an evil act, and God is Jehovah-Urizen, like the figure on the title page of *Europe*. His "creation" of man consists in reducing him from the life of infinity to the restricted and finite life of this world, which is symbolised by the serpent wound round the leg of Adam, the regular symbol in Blake for materialism.

The next three prints deal with the Fall and its immediate consequences. The subject of *Satan Exulting over Eve,* though very rare, is self-ex-

[14] This is usually called the *Elohim Creating Adam,* but on the only occasion when Blake refers to the print he gives it the simpler title *God Creating Adam.*

planatory, and the lost print of *God Judging Adam,* mentioned by Blake in a letter,[15] dealt with a moment preliminary to the expulsion from Eden, a theme more traditional in European painting.

Next comes another very rare biblical subject, *Lamech and his Two Wives.* As told in the fourth chapter of Genesis the story is almost unintelligible, but the one point that emerges clearly, the fact that Lamech killed a man, is evidently Blake's central theme and, like the *Death of Abel,* which Blake later treated in Tempera and water-colour, symbolises death as one of the consequences of the Fall.

Another result of the Fall, sickness and suffering, is the theme of the *Lazar House* (Plate 27a), though in this case Blake has turned to Milton rather than to the Bible itself. In the eleventh book of *Paradise Lost* Michael shows to Adam the consequences of his action, first death in the story of Cain and Abel, then sickness and suffering in the celebrated description of the Lazar House.

Another print not taken directly from the Bible seems to develop a parallel theme. This is the composition of *Hecate.* (Plate 26a). This print is usually said to illustrate either *Macbeth* (Act iii, scene 5, or Act iv, scene 1) or Puck's last speech in *A Midsummer Night's Dream,* but in fact it bears very little resemblance to either description, except for the fact that in Puck's speech she is referred to as "triple Hecate" and is so depicted by Blake. In the print she is surrounded by evil-looking creatures —a donkey, eating thistle leaves with serrated edges like bat's wings (always a symbol of evil with Blake), an owl, and an animal of which only the head is visible but which looks like some enormous lizard— while over her head hovers a still more alarming creature with a devilish face and bat's wings. Hecate herself has her hand on an open book. She seems in fact to be depicted as the goddess of necromancy, a func-

15 *Letters of William Blake,* ed. by Keynes, p. 150.

tion which she regularly performed in Antiquity.[16] In this case the print would represent superstition, another aspect of the domination of Urizen in this case through the priesthood of established religion.

If this interpretation is correct, the *Newton* (Plate 30c) and the *Nebuchadnezzar* (Plate 31c) would form a sort of trilogy with *Hecate*. Newton is a character regularly quoted by Blake, together with Locke, as the exponent of Urizen's religion of reason on earth. The figure of Newton is shown seated at the bottom of the sea and holding the compasses, both details which relate the figure to Urizen, one to his appearance on the frontispiece to *Europe,* the other to the plate in *Urizen* which shows him submerged in the waters of materialism. *Nebuchadnezzar* symbolises the further stage of man's degradation. Newton shows him abandoning imagination in favour of reason only; in Nebuchadnezzar reason has vanished and man has submitted himself wholly to the dictates of the senses.[17]

The print called *Pity* (Plate 28a) is more allusive. It illustrates very precisely the lines in *Macbeth:*

> And pity, like a naked new-born babe,
> Striding the blast, or heaven's cherubin, hors'd
> Upon the sightless Couriers of the air,
> Shall blow the horrid deed in every eye,
> That tears shall drown the wind.

[16] Blake's views on magic and miracles are set forth in one of his marginal notes to Bishop Watson's *Apology,* written in 1798, three years after the *Hecate* was made, and it is possible that in the *Hecate* he is attacking what he considered the false conception of a miracle, asserted by Watson and "the priests" as "an arbitrary act of the agent upon an unbelieving patient," an idea which he contrasted with Christ's conception of a miracle as something based on faith.

[17] The *Nebuchadnezzar* is evidently intended as an exact pendant to the *Newton,* and the parallel probably extends to the settings. The background of the *Nebuchadnezzar* is not easy to decipher, but in the *Marriage of Heaven and Hell* he is shown against tree trunks, which would appropriately signify the vegetative universe, and the woven forms behind the king in the big print may well be leaves, which would have the same symbolism.

It may be connected with Enitharmon, one of the figures in Blake's private mythology, who is identified with pity and the female principle. Enitharmon came into existence at one of the stages in the division of the united fourfold man, which mark the Fall of man from his infinite existence. She was given off by Los and became his emanation. According to Blake she dominated one early phase of history of mankind and so would fit into the series telling this story.

In *Ruth* Blake comes back to the Bible but is probably still dealing with the same theme. The story of Ruth refusing to leave her mother-in-law Naomi, while Orpah returns to Moab, is an obvious illustration for the theme of pity, and since the story is entirely enacted by women, it would fit in well with Blake's identification of pity with the female principle.

The relation of the *Elijah* (Plate 28*b*) to the whole group is slightly different. For Blake the prophets of the Old Testament were, like the poets of later times, the embodiment of the imagination, and the story of Elijah going up to heaven in the chariot of fire, an obvious symbol for the chariot of inspiration, and letting his mantle fall on Elisha, is clearly intended to bring out the continuity of the poetic tradition. The tone of the composition, however, is one of gloom, and it must be taken to indicate the unhappy position of the poet in a world dominated by Jehovah-Urizen and a society governed by the restrictive rules of his servant Moses. There may be a hope implicit in this design, but it is overshadowed by the tragedy of the poet's existence, which is a clear reflection of Blake's own position at this time.

The last print is the most obscure. In a letter already quoted Blake simply calls it "Good and Evil Angel" (Plate 32*b*). It has been called *Los, Enitharmon and Orc* (Orc being the son of Los and Enitharmon and the spirit of revolution) and this may possibly be correct, though if so, it is puzzling that Blake should have referred to it only by a simplified title when writing to Butts. But in any case it certainly represents one aspect of the tragedy of man under the old dispensation. The male figure on the left, flying outwards against a background of flames, but chained by one foot and blind, must symbolise in some form energy or imagination restrained by reason. The design is a development of a crude illustration in the *Marriage of Heaven and Hell,* but there also its meaning is, unfortunately, obscure.

This series of prints must be regarded as the most magnificent expression of the ideas expounded by Blake in the Lambeth Books. They are far more impressive than any of the illustrations to the books themselves, for they have a grandeur and a simplicity which Blake hardly ever attained on the smaller scale of his copper plates—the one exception is the frontispiece to *Europe*—and a clarity of design which is rare in his work before this time. The effectiveness of the prints is partly due to the very simple scaffolding of the compositions: the repeated horizontals of *Pity* and *Satan Exulting over Eve,* the semi-circle of the sun behind the *God Creating Adam,* the quadrant of the chariot of fire in *Elijah,* or the symmetry of the figure of Death in the *Lazar House.* The monotony and emptiness which might result from the use of such simple methods are avoided by means of the great richness of texture produced by Blake's special technique and the elaboration of details within the main scaffolding. The result is a combination of intensity and control rare in Blake's work, and it could be argued that from a purely artistic point of view these are his most successful compositions.

At about the same time Blake made a series of small prints of great beauty, now in the British Museum, which were produced by a combination of the methods used in the printed books and the monotype process used for the big prints. These small prints are pulled from the metal plates of pages from the Lambeth Books (Plates 20*a*, 20*b*), but from the illustrations only, without any text. They also differ from the corresponding plates in the books in that the full colouring was applied to the plate, as was the case in the big prints, so that the rich and mottled texture obtained by this method is used over the whole surface and not only for the outline, as is normally the case with the books themselves. The result is an effect of gem-like beauty never to be found in the books, and the pages of *Thel,* for instance, take on a quite new intensity of colour. The coloured print of *Glad Day* (Plate 1) was made by the same process, but its gaiety and its more optimistic theme suggest that it was made later, probably after 1800, when Blake was beginning to emerge from the despondency of the Lambeth period.

During the 1790s Blake's procedure as a painter changed fundamentally. In the first half of the decade his finest work consisted of the illustrations to the pages of his books. As has already been said, these take on an increasing importance till in the later Lambeth Books they frequently occupy the whole page to the exclusion of the text. In the colour-print series of 1795 he goes a step further and produces for the first time a series of compositions which are not related to any text, but which form the continuous exposition of a philosophical theme. From this time onwards Blake was to make increasingly frequent use of this method, though the colour-prints of 1795 are in one respect unique. The other series of drawings, paintings, water-colours, or engravings always illustrate a particular work—the Bible or one of the poets whom Blake admired; but in the 1795 set he seems to have chosen themes from various different sources—the Bible, Milton, Shakespeare, and English history—all of which were adaptable to the particular philosophical theme that interested him at that moment.

5. The Illustrations to the Bible and to Milton

THE YEARS from 1795 to 1800 were devoted mainly to the composition of the long poem *Vala,* which was never completed and exists only in manuscript. This seems to have absorbed the greater part of Blake's creative energy, and in the visual arts he produced little of real originality. His main work was for publishers. In 1796–97 he made more than 500 water-colours for an edition of Young's *Night Thoughts,* commissioned by Edwards, an enterprising bookseller (Plate 54*b*); but only one part appeared, and its small success prevented the project from being continued. It is not one of Blake's more successful sets of inventions. The idea of filling the page with figures covering the wide margins into which the text of the poems is set is ingenious, but the forms often repeat those he had used earlier for his own compositions on a smaller scale, and they lose greatly by being inflated to fill the folio pages, since they are not worked up with the precision of detail and richness of texture which contribute so much to the success of the big colour-prints.[1]

Much more significant and much more successful is the series of tempera paintings of Biblical subjects which Blake executed in the years

[1] Blake used the same method in his water-colour designs to Gray, also made during the Lambeth years. The illustrations to Young undoubtedly contain personal interpretations added to the text by Blake, but no analysis of them has so far been published, though one was undertaken by Albert S. Roe on the same lines as his work on the Dante drawings.

1799–1800 for his friend and patron Thomas Butts.[2] These paintings are executed in the technique which Blake called "fresco" and which, he declared, was infinitely superior to the hated oil painting. It is in fact a variant of the tempera medium, but Blake probably used carpenter's glue instead of egg, with the result that, contrary to his hopes and predictions, the paintings have darkened and flaked more than his other works and more than contemporary works in oils. In recent years, however, many of them have been restored with success and have regained much of their original beauty.

The mood of this series, as indicated by the choice of subject, is entirely different from that of the colour-prints of 1795. It may have been out of deference to the taste of Butts, who probably did not feel at home in Blake's mythological world, that the artist chose all his themes from the Bible, but the actual selection of them is certainly his own personal choice. Of the thirty-seven compositions which appear to have made up the series, eight illustrate the Old Testament and twenty-nine the New. Of the first eight some, like the *Sacrifice of Isaac* and *Moses in the Ark of Bullrushes,* are traditional foreshadowings of salvation, while the *Judgement of Solomon,* normally a symbol of justice, could equally well be one of true maternal love, a theme which was close to Blake's heart and which reappears in the *Rachel.* It is certainly not a matter of chance that five of the Old Testament compositions deal with questions of woman and conventional morality. *Susanna* is as clear a protest against hypocrisy in such matters as *Jane Shore* had been twenty years earlier; *Lot and His Daughters* and *Bathsheba* (Plate 34a) may well have been chosen to illustrate the point that even the noblest figures of the Old Testament broke the laws of their own religion in sexual matters. They reflect an idea expressed in the *Marriage of Heaven and Hell:* "Jesus Christ is the greatest man, you ought to love him in the greatest degree;

[2] The full list of subjects illustrated in this series is given in Appendix B.

now hear how he has given his sanction to the ten commandments: did
he not . . . turn away the law from the woman taken in adultery. . . .
Jesus was all virtue, and acted from impulse not from rules." [3] The story
of Samson may illustrate the dominance of woman, Delilah personifying
Enitharmon and Samson being Los, the spirit of energy which the female
principle seeks to subdue. *Esther* reveals the opposite aspect of the function of woman and is also a well-known antitype of salvation.

Nine of the New Testament subjects deal with the childhood of
Christ, and they include themes such as the *Christ Child Riding on a
Lamb* and the *Christ Child Asleep on the Cross* (Plate 35*a*), which are
rare in Protestant iconography but relatively common in seventeenth
century Roman Catholic art. The remainder hardly require any explana-
tion: the miracles; Christ blessing little children, an obvious theme for
Blake; a group dealing with the Passion; and a set of the four Evangelists,
significantly of an upright format otherwise used only for the *Moses
Indignant at the Golden Calf,* no doubt to underline the parallel and
contrast between the old and the new dispensations. The series closes
with two more allegorical pieces. *Faith, Hope and Charity* is traditional
in its iconography, but *Christ the Mediator* (Plate 34*b*) illustrates a little-
known sentence of St. Paul: "For there is one God, and one mediator
between God and men, the man Jesus Christ." [4] These words are in
conformity with Blake's oft-repeated doctrine of the identity of God and
man.

Generally speaking, Blake keeps close to the Biblical narrative and even
to conventional renderings of these familiar stories, but in one or two
cases something very personal appears. The group treating of the Passion,
for instance, includes the rare episode of the *Procession from Calvary*
(Plate 33), which is transformed by Blake into a series of figures from a

[3] *Works*, p. 202.   [4] I Timothy II.5.

Gothic cathedral carrying on their shoulders a body which, though naked except for a loincloth, has the stiffness of a thirteenth-century recumbent tomb effigy. The *Agony in the Garden* is original in that the angel, instead of offering the cup, is shown plunging down to support the fainting figure of Christ. Most curious of all, however, is the *Nativity* (Plate 35*b*), in which the Child, radiating light, leaps into the air from the Virgin, supported by St. Joseph, towards the outstretched arms of another woman seated with a baby in her lap, presumably St. Elizabeth with St. John the Baptist. There seems to be no model for this impressive manner of emphasising the miraculous character of the birth of Christ.

The radiance which emanates from the Christ Child in this composition is a feature common to most members of this series. For the first and almost the only time in his life Blake constructs his composition by strong passages of light—almost always of supernatural origin—against a surrounding darkness. In this he might seem to be following the methods of Correggio, or Caravaggio, or Rembrandt, to which he was so strongly opposed, but the effect is closer to that of early fifteenth-century Flemish examples,[5] some of which he may possibly have known.[6]

The light shining in the darkness of these paintings is typical of Blake's state of mind in the years when they were executed. He was beginning to emerge from the gloom of the earlier Lambeth years, and to be less obsessed by the evil of the world. In this series he no longer dwells on pessimistic subjects like the effects of the Fall, but rather on the hopes of salvation created by the incarnation of Christ. *Christ the Mediator* could be taken as summing up the message of the whole series, and this increasing optimism expresses itself not only in the radiance springing from the Christ Child in the *Nativity* but in the lighter and more fluent

[5] For instance, the *Nativity* ascribed to Geertgen in the National Gallery, London.
[6] For Blake's knowledge of fifteenth-century Flemish and German painting, see p. 76.

forms which replace the constricted and frightening designs of the Lambeth Books. But this was only a beginning, and Blake's complete recovery of light was not to be achieved in a moment.

In September of 1800 Blake accepted an invitation from William Hayley to move from London to a cottage on Hayley's estate at Felpham near Chichester. Here he was to stay for more than three years, years which were fruitful both in poetry and in painting but above all important because of Blake's escape from the pessimism of the Lambeth period. In July, shortly before his departure from London, he wrote to George Cumberland: "I begin to emerge from a deep pit of Melancholy", and the overcoming of this state of mind was to continue without interruption during the whole of his stay in Sussex.

Relations with Hayley, a poet of very minor talent with little understanding for the art or the ideas of Blake, soon became difficult, but they did not impede the progress of Blake's recovery of mental health. No doubt the calmer life and clearer atmosphere of the country contributed to his improvement. Blake himself speaks with enthusiasm of his cottage, of which he inserts an engraving in *Milton,* the poem written at Felpham and engraved on his return to London. It is also significant that, while at Felpham, Blake made what seems to have been his only two landscapes from life, one a view of Chichester Cathedral, used in an engraving, the other a view of the old mill, now in the Tate Gallery. The latter shows, incidentally, that Blake's command of the technique of water-colour could have made him successful in landscape painting had he thought it an art worth cultivating.

His recovery, however, was fundamentally due to intellectual rather than physical circumstances. While he was at Felpham his approach to the problems of religion and philosophy changed profoundly, and he gradually abandoned his conviction that the universe was fundamentally evil and that there was little hope of salvation for man.

The change was one of emphasis rather than a reversal of previously held views, but it was not less important for that. Blake still held that the material world was evil and that it limited the life of the imagination, but he began to feel that man's power to break free from these limitations was greater, and, specifically, that this could be done by proper use of the senses. In earlier writings he had usually regarded the senses as connected with materialism and therefore opposed to imagination; now, extending the idea of seeing *through* not *with* the eye, he arrived at his new conception of the fourfold vision, which embraced man in his perfect state before his unity was destroyed by the Fall. In his poem to Butts, included in a letter written just after his arrival at Felpham, he speaks of "My first Vision of Light" after the darkness of Lambeth, and two years later he writes to the same friend another poem ending with the following lines:

> Now I a fourfold vision see,
> And a fourfold vision is given to me;
> 'Tis fourfold in my supreme delight
> And threefold in soft Beulah's night
> And twofold Always. May God us keep
> From Single vision & Newton's sleep! [7]

The first fruits of this new approach towards life are to be seen in the series of water-colours illustrating biblical subjects which Blake executed for Butts while at Felpham and in the years immediately after his return to London. There is little doubt that Blake was here following the same procedure that he had used in the tempera set, but on a far bigger scale, for more than eighty compositions are known to have belonged to it, and of these the greater part still survive. In fact this must have been intended to be "Blake's Bible," just as the loggia frescoes are "Raphael's Bible." It would be imprudent to attribute too precise a significance to the

[7] *Works,* p. 1068.

exact choice of subjects, many of which no doubt had for Blake some private and personal association, but the general trend of the argument is fairly clear. As in the tempera series, the New Testament receives a bigger share than the Old, though twenty-seven are devoted to the latter, and the Gospels are given relatively fewer items, because twelve are allotted to the Apocalypse and, more surprisingly, five to the story of St. Paul.[8]

Of the subjects taken from the Old Testament some, like the *Brazen Serpent*,[9] refer to the tyranny of the Old Dispensation while others bear on the enslavement of the Jews by foreign invaders, as in the *Waters of Babylon*, but even in this case God's revenge is recalled in the succeeding design of the *King of Babylon in Hell*. The theme is more usually the victory over evil, as it is in the *Burial of Moses*, in which the story is told according to the text of Jude 9 with the emphasis on the defeat of the devil, and is so made into a parallel with the *Third Temptation*. Even in the first water-colours, dealing with the Creation and the Fall, Blake is much less despondent than he had been in the Lambeth years and the subjects are *The Creation of Light, God Blessing the Seventh Day*, (Plate 42a), *God Bringing Eve to Adam*, and the *Angel of the Divine Presence Clothing Adam and Eve*, as opposed to the subjects of death and suffering which Blake had selected from this period of man's history for his colour-prints of 1795. Certain of the Old Testament themes prob-

[8] The full list of subjects is given in Appendix B. The dates between which the series was executed are not quite clearly determinable. Of the dated examples all except one are from the years 1803 to 1806, but this one, the *Soldiers Casting Lots*, is dated 1800, and it is likely that Blake started the series in that year, just before his move to Felpham. (Cf. *Works*, p. 1042.)

[9] For a detailed analysis of the significance of this composition, see Blunt, *Journal of the Warburg and Courtauld Institutes*, VI (1943), 225. The Brazen Serpent itself and the two serpents flying through the sky seem to have been taken from Michelangelo's treatment of the same subject in one of the pendentives in the Sistine Chapel. Blake also borrowed from this fresco a crouching figure which he uses on page 13 of *Urizen*. Fuseli had made a variant on this figure in one of his drawings executed in Rome in 1771 (see Schiff, *Zeichnungen*, pp. 6 f.).

ably refer to the part played in man's evolution by the female principle—
Samson, Ruth, and possibly *Jephtha's Daughter;* but here again the main
emphasis is on Blake's familiar attack on hypocrisy and a plea for freedom and forgiveness in sexual matters—*Potiphar's Wife, The Woman
Taken in Adultery,* and *Mary Magdalene Washing Christ's Feet.* Forgiveness is again the theme of the *Pardon of Absolom.* Generally speaking, however, Blake seems to prefer the stories in the Old Testament
which foreshadow the salvation of Christ: *Noah and the Rainbow,
Jacob's Dream* (Plate 44), *Moses and the Burning Bush, Moses Striking
the Rock, David and Goliath,* (Plate 40*b*), *David Delivered out of Many
Waters,* and many others.

Of the New Testament subjects many, as in the tempera series, are
chosen from the childhood of Christ while others illustrate the Miracles,
and one group—perhaps the most dramatic—is devoted to the Passion
(Plates 37*a*, 37*b*). The five drawings illustrating the acts of St. Paul
include two of the saint throwing off the viper, a subject which Blake
certainly saw as the triumph over the serpent of evil and materialism,
and the series ends with twelve drawings of the Apocalypse (Plates 38*a*,
38*b*, 39*a*), a book to which Blake paid increasing attention during his
later years.[10]

Generally speaking, although some of these subjects are rarely represented in painting, there is nothing exceptional about Blake's versions
of them; but in one or two cases he introduces unusual elements. Sometimes these are adapted from traditional allegorical ideas, as, for instance,

---

[10] One group of compositions, *Plague, Pestilence,* and *Famine,* seems to refer not to
the Bible but to the Litany, although for *Pestilence* (Plate 40*a*) Blake has chosen a theme
from the Old Testament, the death of the first-born. It is possible that the water-colour
usually called *Fire* may also be based on the Litany and symbolise "lightning and tempest,"
and that the lost composition *War* (Rossetti, No. 227) may stand for "battle, murder
and sudden death." These themes had been linked by Blake in an early water-colour,
now lost but recorded as being exhibited in the Royal Academy of 1780: *War Unchained
by an Angel—Fire, Pestilence and Famine following.*

when he shows the pelican feeding her young (a common symbol for Charity) in the foreground of the *Finding of Moses,* the connection being emphasised by the subtitle that he gives to the composition: *The Compassion of Pharaoh's Daughter.* Others, like the *Infant Jesus Saying His Prayers,* are personal to Blake, but within the framework of the Christian tradition. In a few cases, however, he intermingles his own symbolism with that of the Bible, as in the *David and Goliath* (Plate 40*b*), in which the shield of the giant bears a scaly monster of serpent-like form and with a bearded human head, clearly symbolising the evil tyranny of Urizen through the Philistines in truly Blakean terms; or in *Christ in the Carpenter's Shop* where the Christ Child holds a pair of dividers like those held by Urizen-Jehovah in the frontispiece to *Europe,* the meaning being in this case that in the new dispensation reason, symbolised by the mathematical instrument, will be synthesised with imagination, just as the old law is synthesised with the new law of the Gospel.[11]

In this series of bliblical illustrations Blake's range of expression is greater than before. He can still play on horrors, as in the *Stoning of Achan* (Plate 36*a*); he can be dramatic, as in the *Soldiers Casting Lots* (Plate 37*a*), with its brilliant inversion of the normal order, so that the crosses are seen in the background and from behind and the foreground is filled with the evil-looking soldiers; he can be apocalyptic, as in the *Great Red Dragon* (Plate 38*a*), or he can reach to the extremes of sweetness, as in the *River of Life* (Plate 38*b*); and his style goes through an equally great range of variations.

It would be possible to describe this phase of Blake's art as Mannerist in a fairly strict sense of the word, but one would have at once to add that he used almost every form which the style took on in order to find an appropriate expression for his subject. In the grimmer subjects, like

[11] Blunt, *Journal of the Warburg Institute* II (1938–9), 60.

the *Achan,* he gives his figures thickset proportions and muscular forms based on the tragic style of the late Michelangelo. In the *River of Life,* on the other hand, the heads are about a tenth of the height of the bodies which are drawn out into forms as exaggerated as those of Parmigiano but resembling more closely the elongations employed by some artists of the late eighteenth century, such as Stothard, whom one could describe as neo-Mannerist. Blake uses these proportions for the purpose for which they were invented, to give a spiritual and ethereal character to the figures and to lift them out of the material world into the world of the imagination.

His colour follows the theme in precisely the same way. In the brutal stories of the Old Testament, showing the domination of Urizen-Jehovah, they are harsh and sombre; in the *River of Life* they complement the lyrical flow of the lines; in *Jacob's Dream* the blue conveys the feeling for the infinite which was vouchsafed to the patriarch in his vision and which was of such vital importance to the painter-poet. Rarely did Blake combine simplicity of colour so happily with boldness of formal invention.

In many of these water-colours the composition is of almost dangerous simplicity, and Blake uses effects of symmetry which sometimes come near to complete failure. But in the *Achan* this method effectively emphasises the horror of the action, while in the *Entombment* it underlines the calm sadness of the moment. Even more effective is the symmetrically posed pair of angels who hover over the dead body of Christ in the composition representing *Christ in the Sepulchre* (Plate 37*b*) forming, as it were, a late Gothic ogee canopy. In other cases Blake uses repetition of forms in a different manner, as in the *Wise and Foolish Virgins,* where the silhouette of the flying angel precisely follows the line of the hills.

As Blake himself tells us, his spiritual development during the three years at Felpham was deeply affected by his study of Milton, after whom he named the long poem which had been his principal interest during that time. The book is not notable for illustrations, except for one or two whole pages such as those containing the symbolical figures of Blake and his brother Robert, but the artist uses a new type of layout which he was to repeat in *Jerusalem,* his last engraved book. In his two last poems Blake used a new metre, the fourteen-foot line, which is longer than any he had previously used, and even the bigger pages of *Milton* and *Jerusalem* do not leave a margin over which the symbolic decorations can be spread as in the earlier volumes. In consequence Blake makes a different disposition of text and plates. As in the Lambeth Books, he includes a certain number of full-page plates without text and some with an illustration at the top or bottom of the page; but the commonest form is a page composed almost entirely of text, with minute figures or decorative motives winding in and out between the lines of the text but taking up very little space. This naturally produces a heavier and less attractive page, but in the few copies which he coloured Blake breaks up the monotony of the effect by a more elaborate use of washes across the whole page.

The effect of the study of Milton is to be found not only in the poem of that name but also in the water-colours illustrating the poet's works, made in the last twenty-five years of Blake's life. His attitude towards Milton was a mixture of admiration and disapproval. He loved the creator of Lucifer, the great rebel, and he admired the hedonist who described the sensuous delights of Adam and Eve in the garden of Eden; but he hated the Puritan moralist who dictated the reproving and repressive speeches of the archangel Raphael. His first series of illustrations to Milton are those for *Paradise Lost,* made for Butts in 1808 and now in the Museum of Fine Arts, Boston (Plates 45, 46*b*, 47), and they throw much light on his feeling for the poet. In the *Downfall of the Rebel Angels* Blake is happy and successful when he is drawing the naked, Michelangelesque figures of the rebels being hurled into the abyss, but he is much less successful in depicting the figure of God who throws them down, and still less so with the angelic choir surrounding him. What Blake said of Milton evidently applied to himself: "the reason Milton wrote in fetters when he wrote of Angels and God, and at liberty when of Devils and Hell, is that he was a true Poet and of the Devil's party without knowing it"—the difference being that Blake was consciously and deliberately of the Devil's party.

Even more striking, however, are the paintings of Adam and Eve in the Garden of Eden. The artist has evolved a quite new technique to give full value in visual form to the descriptions by Milton, whose text he follows scrupulously. The relatively loose forms of the Bible illustrations are replaced by a jewelled precision of detail and an intensity of colour by which Blake contrives to render with the utmost vividness such passages as the description of Eden:

> Groves whose rich trees wept odorous gums and balm,
> Others whose fruit burnish'd with golden rind
> Hung amiable, Hesperian fables true

or individual details such as "the soft downy bank damask'd with flow'rs," or the blossoms which "wrought mosaic" on the bower and "broider'd the ground" under the feet of Adam and Eve. All the illustrations to these scenes from the fourth book of the poem reveal a sensuousness which is quite new in Blake. It is the expression of his new realisation that the senses are not evil, as he had previously felt, but can be used as a means to further the spiritual life, a doctrine towards which he had been led largely by the reading of Milton. Even in subjects such as the *Temptation of Eve* or the *Prophecy of the Crucifixion,* which are more solemn in their implication, Blake still uses the same jewelled effect and so renders them much less sombre than any work that he had produced during the Lambeth years.[12]

[12] In 1809 Blake made for Butts a further set of illustrations to Milton, this time to the *Ode on the Morning of Christ's Nativity* (now in the Whitworth Institute, Manchester; cf. Plate 42c).

From the material point of view the years after Blake's return to London were among the worst of his whole life, but in spite of these difficulties his state of mind continued to improve and his letters sometimes take on an ecstatic tone. In October, 1804, for instance, he writes to Hayley: "Suddenly, on the day after visiting the Truchsessian Gallery of pictures, I was again enlightened with the light I enjoyed in my youth, and which has for exactly twenty years been closed from me as by a door and by window-shutters." And, again, "Dear Sir, excuse my enthusiasm or rather madness, for I am really drunk with intellectual vision whenever I take a pencil or graver into my hand, even as I used to be in my youth, and as I have not been for twenty dark, but very profitable years. I thank God that I courageously pursued my course through darkness." [13] The Truchsessian Gallery referred to in this passage was a collection of paintings formed by a German, Count Joseph Truchsess, which was exhibited in London in 1803. Its importance for Blake was that it included not only works by popular artists of the seventeenth century, but also paintings by German and Flemish painters of the sixteenth century. Later Blake was able to see even more important works of the earlier schools in the house of Charles Aders, who owned paintings attributed to the great names of the fifteenth as well as the sixteenth century,[14] and there is no doubt that the study of these collections had a stimulating effect on Blake's imagination in the last decades of his life.

The years 1805 and 1806 were embittered by the keen disappointment which the artist experienced over what might have been his two best chances of gaining greater popularity with the public: the illustrations to Blair's *Grave* and the engraving of the *Canterbury Pilgrims,* both

[13] *Works,* p. 1108.

[14] An account of this collection is given by Passavant in his *Tour of a German Artist in England,* I (London, 1876), 201 ff. It included a copy of Van Eyck's Ghent altarpiece, now at Antwerp, the *Virgin and Child with Saints* by Petrus Christus, now at Frankfort, as well as paintings attributed to Memling, Antonello da Messina, and Schöngauer.

projects promoted by the publisher Cromek. In the case of the Blair, Cromek commissioned Blake to make designs and promised that he should also have the much more lucrative job of engraving them; but, having got the designs, and realising that Blake's hard manner would not meet with approval from the public, he handed them over to the more popular Schiavonetti, a pupil of Bartolozzi, thereby depriving Blake of his financial reward and transforming the designs into something tame and uninteresting. In the case of the *Canterbury Pilgrims* his behaviour was even more discreditable, for, having seen Blake working on a composition of this subject—one never treated before that time— and having encouraged him to continue with it, Cromek went to Blake's friend Stothard and proposed the theme to him as an original idea of his own, without mentioning the fact that Blake was working on it. In due course Cromek published an engraving after Stothard's painting, with great profit to himself, thereby not only cheating Blake again but in addition breaking up the long friendship between the two artists.

Enraged by this treatment, Blake decided to make a direct bid for the favour of the public, and in 1809 he organised a private exhibition of his work in his brother's house in Broad Street. As would be expected, the exhibition was a total failure and produced neither sales nor publicity. It was, however, the occasion for the production of Blake's *Descriptive Catalogue,* which was sold at the exhibition and contained not only a long and brilliant analysis of Chaucer's poem but also Blake's clearest statements about the nature of his art, many of which have been quoted in a previous chapter. It is on this occasion that he launches his most violent attack on the colour of Rubens and the Venetians, puts up his keenest defence of Raphael and Michelangelo, and expatiates most fully on the merits of his new technique of "fresco."

The exhibition contained only sixteen paintings, of which the most important and the largest was the "fresco" of the *Canterbury Pilgrims,* which Blake was engaged on engraving. The artist also included in it one very early work, the *Penance of Jane Shore,* and four of the biblical water-colours for Butts. Some of the works shown are now lost, but those which are still traceable include the two "frescoes" of *Pitt* and *Nelson* (Plates 46*c*, 46*d*). These are allegories on the subject of War, conceived in apocalyptic terms as the last stage before the Last Judgement. They are among the most obscure of Blake's compositions,[15] and were certainly a strange choice if he intended to capture the patronage of a wide public. But Blake was not a man to compromise and, if the public did not like what he gave them, so much the worse for the public.

[15] For a full discussion of their meaning, see Appendix A.

6. The Last Phase: *Jerusalem,* the Book of Job, and Dante

THE FAILURE of the exhibition of 1809 was a severe blow to Blake, and it was probably owing to this that during the succeeding decade he produced almost no independent paintings, as opposed to book illustrations.[1] In fact, his whole energies seem to have been absorbed in the completion of his long poem *Jerusalem,* which had been begun in 1804 but the engraving of which was probably not finished until about 1818.

As a statement of Blake's final solution to the problems which had haunted him all his life, the poem is of great importance. It embodies his conviction that man can attain salvation by following the doctrine of the Gospel, in practising self-sacrifice and the forgiveness of sins as Christ had practised these virtues. This will free man from the trammels of the material world and will restore him to that state of perfection in which his whole being, divided through the Fall, is reunited. In this state all the contradictions of his divided state are resolved and the forces, such as

[1] The only dated works from these years are two temperas dated 1810 (*Adam Naming the Animals* and the *Virgin in Egypt*); one dated 1811 (the *Spiritual Condition of Man*); and two water-colours of classical subjects, *The Judgement of Paris* and *Philoctetes on Lemnos,* painted for Butts and dated 1811 and 1812 respectively. The last two works are particularly puzzling in view of Blake's scorn for Greek and Roman poets. Presumably the subjects had some special significance for him, and they may, like the *Pitt* and *Nelson,* have been related to the theme of war; the Judgement of Paris was the action that provoked the Trojan War, and the arrival of Philoctetes at Troy led to the death of Paris and the victory of the Greeks.

imagination and reason, which are opposed in his divided state, are harmonised in the final synthesis.

This simple doctrine is given complex and obscure expression in the text and in many of the illustrations, but some passages of the poem, and a few of the plates, rank among Blake's finest achievements.

The general layout of the pages is the same as in *Milton,* with some pages devoted entirely to plates, some to text with only the smallest amount of decoration, and some with an engraved composition occupying the top or the bottom of the page. Certain of the designs are in Blake's most fantastic manner, with bird-headed men gazing at the setting sun, or bat-winged monsters hovering over corpses laid out beside the sea. In one Blake adapts the figure which he had used for the *Stoning of Achan* to an agonised Albion, surrounded by three fate-like females who seem to spin a thread out of his umbilical cord. Another plate shows the chariot drawn by human-headed bulls which has already been mentioned as an instance of Blake's knowledge of Oriental art, and yet another is dominated by the vast arch of Stonehenge, under which walk minute human beings. Others are less sombre, particularly those showing figures seated on a lotus or a lily.

There are, however, two plates which embody superbly the new spirit which inspired Blake at this time: the *Soul Reunited with God* (Plate 49a), and the *Albion and the Crucified Christ* (Plate 48a). The former, which is on the last page of text, is one of Blake's most vehement creations. The ecstasy of the mystic union is conveyed by means of flame-like forms and the rush of one figure towards the other. In it Blake has recovered the curvilinear beauty of the earliest illuminations, but has combined with it the energy of the title page to the *Marriage of Heaven and Hell* and has added a peculiar solemnity derived from his deep and bitter experience during the dark Lambeth years. Innocence is impossible to recapture, but here the artist has expressed the final state to which man can aspire by means of love and imagination after passing through the dark stage of Experience.

Blake seems to have borrowed the idea for the figure group from an engraving by Martin de Vos illustrating the story of the Prodigal Son (Plate 49*b*). Not only are the two characters disposed in a strikingly similar manner, but even the halo surrounding the head of God seems to be adumbrated in the hat of the father in the engraving. The choice of this particular model may not be entirely fortuitous, for the theme of the parable is forgiveness, to which Blake attached such importance at this time, and Samuel Palmer tells us that it was a story that Blake particularly loved and could not read without tears coming to his eyes.[2]

The plate of the *Crucifixion* illustrates one of the culminating passages in the poem, the dialogue between Albion, or Man, and Christ on the Cross, in which Blake sums up his doctrine of self-sacrifice and forgiveness of sins:

> Jesus said: "Wouldest thou love one who never died
> "For thee, or ever die for one who had not died for thee?
> "And if God dieth not for Man & giveth not himself
> "Eternally for Man, Man could not exist; for Man is Love
> "As God is Love: every kindness to another is a little Death
> "In the Divine Image, nor can Man exist but by Brotherhood." [3]

In the design Christ hangs crucified on the Tree of Error, the evil fruits of which are almost concealed by the rays that stream from him. Below stands Albion, in a pose exactly echoing that of the crucified figure, a detail which is meant to emphasise Blake's doctrine of the identity of God and man and also the fact that, to obtain salvation, man must repeat in himself the sacrifice of self and the love of others which are shown forth by Christ in the Crucifixion. Just as in other designs for *Jerusalem* he

---

[2] Gilchrist, *Life of Blake,* p. 302.   [3] *Works,* p. 746.

returns to formal devices which he had employed in his youth, so here he uses a figure which he had invented in 1780 to signify the rising sun and had revived, probably after 1800, for the coloured engraving known as *Glad Day* (cf. Plates 6 and 7). The theme of the *Crucifixion* is still close to the idea underlying the engraving, for below the latter he had inscribed the lines:

> Albion arose from where he labour'd at the Mill with slaves:
> Giving himself for the Nations he danc'd the dance of Eternal Death [4]

which signify the sacrifice which man makes of himself in imitation of the sacrifice of Christ.

The great works of Blake's last years are the designs for the *Book of Job* and the water-colours to Dante, but before discussing them mention must be made of certain minor productions, two of which stand to some extent apart from the artist's main development. These are the *Visionary Heads* and the illustrations to Thornton's *Pastorals*. The former, made in the years 1819 and 1820 for John Varley, have already been mentioned in connection with the nature of Blake's visions.[5] They are curious rather than successful. Some of them represent familiar historical figures, the mediaeval kings and queens of England, classical characters such as Socrates, or biblical personages such as Solomon. Others are more eccentric: *The Man who Built the Pyramids, The Man who Instructed Mr. Blake in Painting in his Dreams,* and, most famous of all, *The Ghost of a Flea.*[6] This last head has a close resemblance to an engraving of a flea in Robert Hooke's *Micrographia,*[7] which Blake almost certainly knew, but it is also strikingly like certain monsters which appear as devils in sixteenth-century Italian painting.[8]

---

[4] *Ibid.,* p. 889.   [5] See above, p. 24.

[6] For a full list, see Gilchrist, *Life of Blake,* pp. 467–70.

[7] See Singer, "The first English microscopist: Robert Hooke," *Endeavour,* XIV (1955), 14.

[8] The closest parallel known to me is in a painting of the *Crucifixion* (Florentine

The illustrations to Thornton's *Pastorals,* made in 1820–21, were Blake's one experiment in woodcutting. They have little in common with his other works and would hardly be remembered for their own sake, but they exercised a profound influence on the small group of young artists who gathered around Blake in his last years, most particularly on Samuel Palmer and Edward Calvert. They saw in them a new and visionary approach to landscape and a means of bursting through the naturalism of the school in which they had been trained, and for some crucial years of their lives their art was dominated by these poetical but slight works, to which one can hardly imagine that Blake himself attached great importance.

In addition to these "eccentric" productions Blake continued during his last years to make illustrations to the works of other writers, particularly Milton. The water-colours to *Paradise Regained, L'Allegro,* and *Il Penseroso* are in a gentler and more lyrical style than those for *Paradise Lost,* but they lack the crisp and precise brilliance of the latter. A set of designs illustrating the *Pilgrim's Progress,* discovered during the war, contain highly personal interpretations of the story, but they are strangely clumsy in drawing and execution. Far greater control and far greater formal invention are to be found in the drawings to the Book of Enoch, which must date from after 1821,[9] and in the two late tempera paintings, *Satan Smiting Job,* now in the Tate, and *Sea of Time and Space,* dated 1821 and now belonging to the National Trust, which is closely based on Porphyry and is the latest instance of Blake's direct debt to neo-Platonism.[10]

The Book of Job was a work which had interested Blake since the

---

School, about 1550), now in the Museum at Aix-en-Provence. Blake could not have known this, but he may have been acquainted with some similar creature in an engraving of the period.

[9] See Brown, *Burlington Magazine,* LXXVII (1940), 80–84.

[10] For a full account of the meaning of this painting, see Raine, *Journal of the Warburg and Courtauld Institutes,* XX (1957), 318–37.

early 1790s, and he had at intervals returned to it as a theme for his paintings, but it was not till the last years of his life that he turned it into a major vehicle for the expression of his ideas in the series of designs called the *Illustrations of the Book of Job* (Plates 52, 53, 55, 56). It is not known exactly when Blake executed the first version of these designs, the water-colours acquired by Butts, but the evidence suggests a date about 1818–20. The second set of water-colours, drawn by Linnell and coloured by Blake, can be firmly dated to 1821, and the engravings to the years 1823–25.[11]

In producing these designs Blake followed his usual practise and adapted the text which he was illustrating to fit his own ideas. His meaning is made plain in certain variations from the Bible version in the actual engravings and, more explicitly, in the texts with which he fills the borders round the figure compositions.[12] In the Bible the Book of Job is a statement of the problem of human suffering, but one which offers no solution to the mystery. Job, a just and upright man, suffers at the hand of God for reasons that he cannot comprehend, and the author offers no answer to his questionings, except that he was wrong in attempting to penetrate the mystery of suffering. The mystery itself is, therefore, left as obscure at the end of the book as at the beginning. To Blake this version evidently seemed unsatisfactory, and he made his own glosses on it. For him Job sinned because, although he followed literally the instructions of the law of Moses, he did so with complacency and without love. This central point is made clear in the text below the first plate (Plate 52 *a*): "The Letter Killeth. The Spirit giveth Life." This theme is further emphasised in the Plate in which Job is shown giving bread to a beggar, and the text reads: "Did I not weep for him who was

---

[11] For a full discussion of the *Book of Job* illustrations, see the publication of them by the Pierpont Morgan Library (1935), with an introduction by Sir Geoffrey Keynes.

[12] Blake's real meaning has been admirably analysed and interpreted by Wicksteed in *Blake's Vision of the Book of Job*.

in trouble? Was not my Soul afflicted for the Poor?" It was this following of orthodox established religion instead of the true doctrine of love
that brought on Job the disasters which are depicted in two plates, the
destruction of his sons and daughters (Plate 52*b*), and Satan smiting him
with sore boils (Plate 55*a*). Then there appear the three comforters,
whose function it is by their hypocrisy to make Job's error so visible
that he begins to be aware of it himself. The real revelation, however,
is brought about by the speech of Elihu beginning with the words: "I am
Young and ye are very Old, wherefore I was afraid", in which he attacks
both the comforters and Job himself and presents the true cause of
Job's suffering (Plate 56*a*). It is typical of Blake that it should be the
young man who first comes to realise the truth and who opens the
eyes of the old. From this point onwards the tone of the book changes,
and Job experiences a series of visions in which the meaning of the
world and man's true place in it are revealed. In one Satan is cast out;
in the next God blesses Job and his wife, while the comforters cower
in terror in the background; and the climax is depicted in the plate in
which Job, standing in the attitude of Albion before the crucified Christ,
offers a sacrifice for himself and for his friends, so bringing forth Blake's
doctrine of love even for an evil neighbour, which had been one of the
central themes of *Jerusalem*. The remaining plates illustrate the restora-
tion of Job to happiness after his trial at the hand of God.

The *Illustrations of the Book of Job* are Blake's most conventional
productions in the visual arts. Technically they are straightforward line-
engravings, and although the combination of text and illustrations is less
usual, it is not unique and it is much simpler than the layout of the
Prophetic Books. In style, moreover, Blake has given up the use of those
Mannerist effects which were so marked in the biblical series of water-
colours. The proportions of the figures are now normal, and the designs
are simple and straightforward. But to say that they are conventional

does not mean that they are not original. It could, on the contrary, be argued that the very fact that they are less eccentric than most of Blake's productions gives them a sort of universality which is lacking in his other works. For once he has reduced his visions to terms which are readily intelligible to all, and they have gained, not lost, in the process. It is no matter of chance that the *Book of Job* should have been known and admired at times when the rest of Blake's works were thought to be the ravings of a lunatic.

In technique the engravings are masterly. As we know from Gilchrist, Blake had refreshed his mind and his hand by a renewed study of the engravings of Marcantonio and Dürer, which he loved from childhood, and his graver takes on a new subtlety and produces a great variety of effects which he had hardly ever achieved in the earlier dry manner learnt from his master Basire. The outline remains as firm as ever, but the modelling is fuller, the effects of light more varied, and the texture richer, so that the absence of colour is more than made up for; and the engravings have a concentration and a force lacking in the preliminary water-colours. The variety of mood is as great as in earlier works, but is achieved by moderate means. The horrors are the more impressive for being stated without the grotesque brutality of *Urizen,* witness Plate 3, the destruction of Job's sons and daughters by fire from Heaven. The night sky shown in the plate of *Elihu* reminds one of the Thornton woodcuts, but it is more solemn because of the simplicity of the means by which it is rendered. Ecstasy is given its most splendid expression in the famous plate *When the Morning Stars Sang Together* (Plate 53*b*).

This last plate was Blake's final statement of a formal theme on which he had made many variations and which derived ultimately from a crude engraving of a relief from Persepolis in Bryant's *New System of Ancient Mythology,* published in 1776 (Plate 54*a*),[13] the row of figures standing

[13] See Keynes, *Blake Studies,* p. 44.

with their arms stretched upwards and overlapping. This device had appeared in one of the illustrations to Young's *Night Thoughts* (Plate 54*b*), where the figures are cherubim with six wings, four of which cover their bodies and legs. The *Job* water-colours show four figures, with one pair of wings each, clad in short skirts and flanked by two wisps of cloud. In the engravings the group is made more coherent and more lively by the introduction of flowing gauze-like dresses which cover the figures right down to their feet and link up with the lines of the clouds, integrating them into the design. But Blake's most effective change in this stage is to add, at each end of the row of figures, an extra arm cut off by the edge of the plate, which suggests with striking effect that the row is continued indefinitely beyond the frame of the engraving and adds mystery to the whole conception.

The *Illustrations of the Book of Job* were Blake's last experiment in the combination of text and figures, and they present a new and remarkably mature solution to this problem. The page is dominated by the central engraving, but this is complemented by the designs in the margins, which are interwoven with texts either from the Book of Job itself, or from some other book of the Bible which Blake thought relevant to his theme. The result could be regarded as an inversion of the method used in the plates to Young and Gray, where the central space is occupied by the text and the illustration is fitted round it. In the *Job* the fusion of the two elements is more complete and successful than in any other illustrated work by Blake.

The last three years of Blake's life were devoted almost exclusively to the vast project of illustrating Dante's *Divine Comedy* (Plates 58–64). In this short time Blake made more than a hundred water-colours, of which he had engraved six at the time of his death in 1827. Artistically these designs represent his last will and testament.

Blake's enthusiasm for Dante is puzzling, for in many and important respects he disapproved of the doctrines set forth in the *Divine Comedy*. In particular Dante's belief in divine retribution, which is fundamental to the whole poem, was directly opposed to Blake's doctrine of redemption through forgiveness; and from certain recorded comments, as well as from notes written on the drawings themselves, we can see how sharp was his opposition to the poet whom he had chosen to illustrate. "Everything in Dante's Comedia shews That for Tyrannical Purposes he has made This World the Foundation of All, and the Goddess Nature Mistress; Nature is his Inspirer and not the Holy Ghost," he wrote on one drawing, and Crabb Robinson records him as saying of Dante: "He was an 'Atheist,' a mere politician busied about this world." [14] It is true, as Mr. Roe has pointed out, that in the water-colours Blake introduces a number of variations from the text of Dante [15] and so in a sense follows the same principle as in the *Book of Job*. But the parallel is not complete, for in the case of *Job* only a small change was necessary to bring the whole story into line with Blake's ideas, whereas with Dante the differences are basic, and many of them are allowed to remain un-amended in the illustrations, particularly in those based on the more savage passages in the *Inferno*.

It is also true, as has often been pointed out, that Blake admired Dante as a poet and a visionary and felt that he was one of those through whom the Poetic Genius had manifested itself; but this is not a sufficient answer to the problem, for to Blake it was essential that a poem should expound a doctrine in accordance with imaginative truth, and this he could not have felt about great parts of the *Divine Comedy*. At most one can say that Blake must have sympathised with Dante's aim of writing

[14] Roe, *Blake's Illustrations to the Divine Comedy*, p. 33. Mr. Roe gives the most detailed account available of the Dante drawings.

[15] Mr. Roe analyses these variations and the meanings which Blake added to Dante with great ingenuity. It is possible to feel that in certain cases he has read into the drawings complications which the artist did not intend, but in general critics have accepted his analysis.

in epic terms about the problems of the universe, and felt that the intensity of his visions placed him with the elect among the poets; but the conflict between the two was fundamental, and the problem why Blake chose this text for his last cycle of illustrations remains a mystery.

The drawings themselves vary in character and in quality. Some are very highly finished, others are hardly begun; some are in Blake's most lucid and mature manner, others are confused and difficult to decipher; some are of intense visionary power, others are almost comic and carry little conviction.

The finished sheets, on which alone it is fair to base a judgment of the whole series, are in a technique new in Blake's work. He began by laying in the main design in the broad washes which are traditional in the medium, and which he had employed in the biblical water-colours for Butts, but he then worked over the whole surface in a series of small touches, almost as if he was painting in tempera, frequently going over the same area many times. The result is an effect of greater richness than in the earlier works in the medium, but the miracle is that Blake manages to avoid the messiness which normally comes with working over the same part several times in water-colour. The different touches are superimposed, so that the upper ones do not disturb the freshness of the lower layers. The artist must have taken the greatest care not to add one touch until the lower layer had completely dried, and he probably used his paint as dry as possible. The effect is one rarely to be seen in water-colour, though it has, curiously enough, a close parallel in the later water-colours of Cézanne.

The formal means used in the Dante water-colours are of great variety. Sometimes Blake boldly creates the impression of infinite space, as in the *Angelic Boat Wafting Souls over for Purgation* (No. 72); in others, such as *Homer and the Ancient Poets* (No. 8), an effect of great scale is achieved, though in fact the cliffs and mountains are no more than six times the height of the figures standing on them. Sometimes Blake plays on the exact repetition of a form, as in *Caiaphas and the Hypocrites* (Plate 61*a*), or the *Inscription over Hell Gate* (Plate 58*a*). Sometimes his boldness is almost alarming, as in the *Antaeus* (Plate 59*a*), where he uses every possible means to bring out the colossal size of the giant. The effectiveness of this design can be best seen by a comparison with Flaxman's tidy neoclassical version of the same scene (Plate 59*b*). Flaxman shows the giant in a crouching posture, so that his size is minimised in comparison with the two poets and he forms a compact block-like form. Blake sets him in the most cumbersome pose, hanging precariously on a ledge of the cliff and sprawling across the page, one vast hand just setting down Virgil, a puny figure no bigger than the hand itself.

Among the finest and most complete of the illustrations to the *Inferno* are the *Simoniac Pope* (Plate 58*b*) and the *Circle of the Lustful* (Plate 60*a*). In the former Blake has used his new technique to brilliant effect in rendering the molten cloud and the transparent glowing well in which the pope is poised, head downwards; but in addition he has created a design striking by its very simplicity: a figure eight enveloping the pope in its lower half and in the upper part enclosing the figure of Virgil sweeping Dante away from the horrific sight. The same impression of rushing motion is achieved in the *Circle of the Lustful,* but on an even larger scale, for the whole design is dominated by the spiral curve of the flame which sweeps the lustful up out of the river while a smaller flame in the background carries off Paolo and Francesca. Here the effect of motion is intensified by the contrast with the static group on the right: the standing figure of Virgil, the fainting Dante prostrate at his feet, and the vision of the lovers at their first meeting, shown in a sun over the two poets.

Somewhat surprisingly Blake devoted more drawings to the *Inferno* than to the *Purgatorio* and the *Paradiso* together, though it must be remembered that the series was left incomplete and the artist may have intended to add further designs for the later parts of the poem. In any case, the quality of the best *Purgatorio* drawings is as high as any in the whole series. *Lucia Carrying Dante in His Sleep* (Plate 60*b*) is a vision of night even more magical than the *Elihu* plate from *Job,* and in the two water-colours of *Beatrice in the Car* (Plates 62, 63) Blake reaches new heights both in technique and in the rendering of a visionary experience. His rainbow colours are the ideal vehicle to express the poet's ecstasy at the moment of reunion with Beatrice.

Of the *Paradiso* designs few are finished, but they include one group which shows Blake for once in complete harmony with his subject. In Canto xxiv Dante is questioned first by St. Peter concerning Faith, then by St. James about Hope, and finally by St. John on Love. Blake has represented all these three scenes, which form a sort of progression to the final design in which St. John flies down towards Dante and Beatrice, while St. James and St. Peter kneel on either side (Plate 64*a*). This, as Mr. Roe has pointed out, must have signified for Blake the recovery of the state of Eden, in which man will overcome the divisions to which he had been subjected in the material world and recover his fourfold unity; and it is, of course, characteristic of Blake that this final synthesis should be attained through Love, of which St. John is the symbol. To express this unity, Blake has used a formula common in mediaeval manuscripts and stained glass, in which figures are depicted in overlapping roundels (Plate 64*b*). So, at the very end of his life, the artist returns to that Gothic art which he had studied as a child in Westminster Abbey.[16]

Having examined the characteristics of Blake as an artist and followed the development of his style and means of expression there remains the

[16] Blake may have known a manuscript like that in Plate 64*b,* and there was in his day a window in the northeast transept of Canterbury Cathedral showing, round a central square panel, four semicircular panels with single figures of prophets. This would come near to the formula used by Blake.

task of trying to assess his achievement in the field of painting and engraving. Such an assessment is exceptionally difficult, because Blake as a man, as a thinker, as a poet, and as an artist arouses dangerously strong feelings, with the result that it is rare to hear moderate judgements of him. Few would now take up the nineteenth-century attitude that he was mad; and anyone who studies his work carefully will be bound to conclude that his doctrines, though often obscure, are perfectly consistent and that they belong to a long tradition of mysticism from which Blake himself claimed descent. But this is as far as agreement would go. To some he is a unique phenomenon, a prophet who discovered the truth and conveyed it to the world in its most resplendent form by means of his poems and his designs. To others he is an unbalanced fanatic, obsessed by eccentric ideas which inspired shapeless poems and ill-drawn compositions.

About the merits of his early lyric poetry there would be almost universal agreement; about his Prophetic Books there would be more divergence of opinion, but only the real Blake enthusiast—or should one say Blake maniac?—would maintain that, apart from their importance as the expression of religious and philosophical ideas, they rank high as pure poetry. With the paintings the problem is harder. Their effect is much more direct than that of the poems; for some people it amounts almost to a kind of revelation, but to others it is no more than a shudder at the grimness of some designs or a feeling of nausea at the sweetness of others. In every case, however, the feeling, whether pleasurable or painful, is too strong to be ignored. The force behind the designs is undeniable, but was the artist capable of giving it complete and satisfying expression?

In attempting to answer this question it is important to remember what Blake was aiming at in his painting: to convey through forms and colours his imaginative conception of a particular kind of religious truth.

He therefore belongs to the great family of religious artists, but to a
rather special branch of it, one which did not come into existence till a
late stage in history. The peculiarity of his position in comparison with
the great religious artists of the past—the sculptors of Chartres, the build-
ers of the temples of India or Egypt, the Italian painters of the Trecento
—is that the latter expressed a body of ideas generally accepted by the
society in which they lived, whereas Blake worked in isolation.

At a time when progressive thought was harnessed to the chariot of
reason and science Blake stood for imagination and inspired belief. True,
he was not alone in resisting the claims of reason; in this he was in
agreement with the Romantics and all those who were revolting against
materialism. But the reaction of his contemporaries against reason usually
led them to pantheism or to some form of belief in which a personal
Christian God played little part. Blake was unique among the English
writers of his generation in basing his philosophy solely on Christianity.
His interpretation of the creed may have been unusual and personal,
but his belief in the doctrine of the Gospel was the foundation of his
whole life and thought.

Blake's position as a minority fighter—and in a minority of one for
the greater part of his life—was a source of both strength and weakness
for him. The courage with which he defied the world manifests itself
in the vitality which is so marked a feature of his thought and his art,
and in a refusal to compromise, to blur the edge of an idea or a form,
which makes his best work in poetry or painting so immediately ar-
resting. But this isolation had its dangers. Lacking sympathetic criticism or even the opportunity for constructive discussion, Blake was
driven more and more in on himself; there was no brake to restrain
him and he developed his ideas with ever increasing intensity, in forms
which became more and more personal and less and less intelligible to
others. As with the hero of Balzac's *Chef-d'œuvre inconnu* the search for

the precise expression of his ideal, irrespective of what others might think of it, led to confusion in his writings and eccentricity in his paintings.

But this is not the whole problem. Arthur Symons in his book on Blake tells how he once showed some drawings by the artist to Rodin, and explained: "He used to literally see these figures: they are not mere inventions." "Yes," said Rodin, "he saw them once; he should have seen them three or four times." [17] This, I believe, gets very near the heart of the matter. Blake saw vividly, but he saw schematically. To express what he wanted to convey a series of symbols was often enough, with the result that his works are sometimes *thought* rather than *seen,* whereas with a great visionary painter, like Michelangelo in his later days, the images are as full and as rich visually as they are intellectually.

It would be irrelevant to complain that Blake's paintings are not naturalistic—exact copying of nature would destroy the visionary quality of his work—but if his forms had been based on a real knowledge of the human figure and of its anatomy, on a training in drawing in the best academic sense, they would have a richness and an amplitude which they generally lack.

But if Blake had these weaknesses as a painter he possessed many of the most important qualities which go to make up an artist of genius: passionate conviction, complete integrity of thought and feeling, a fertile visual imagination combined with great invention in design, originality and skill in technique, and above all a vitality and a vehemence which overcome the sometimes insufficient control of form. He may have been a genius *manqué,* but the elements of genius are there.

But these are not the only reasons for the fascination which he exercises over those who admire him. There is a kind of magic in the man, which is impossible to define, but which was strongly felt by those who

[17] *William Blake,* p. 217. Symons took Rodin to mean that Blake noted down his visions immediately and without attempting to develop and improve them, but this, as we have seen, is not the case and was probably not what Rodin meant.

knew him personally. In Samuel Palmer's account of Blake written in 1855, nearly thirty years after the poet's death, this quality comes out vividly:

In him you saw at once the Maker, the Inventor; one of the few in any age: a fitting companion for Dante. He was energy itself, and shed around him a kindling influence; and atmosphere of life, full of the ideal. . . . He was a man without a mask; his aim single, his path straightforwards, and his wants few; so he was free, noble and happy. . . . His eye was the finest I ever saw: brilliant, but not roving, clear and intent, yet susceptible; it flashed with genius, or melted in tenderness. It could also be terrible. Cunning and falsehood quailed under it, but it was never busy with them. It pierced them and turned away. . . .

Such was Blake as I remember him. He was one of the few to be met with in our passage through life, who are not, in some way or other, "double minded" and inconsistent with themselves; one of the very few who cannot be depressed by neglect, and to whose name rank and station could add no lustre. . . . He ennobled poverty, and, by his conversation and the influence of his genius, made two small rooms in Fountain Court more attractive than the threshold of princes.[18]

This magnetic power comes through his writings and his paintings, and it impresses—sometimes even hypnotises—those who study him today.

Blake has also a peculiar relevance in the present age, partly because he faced problems similar to ours. He lived in a period of social upheaval, of revolution and reaction, and in a time which was dominated by the triumph of science and materialism. His complete individualism and his bold defence of personal liberty have clear topical significance today, and his bold assertion of spiritual values has a direct appeal to those who are themselves trying to escape from the dominance of materialism.

But even for those who do not share Blake's religious beliefs his passionate sincerity, his uncompromising integrity, his "hundred-percent"

[18] Quoted by Gilchrist, *Life of Blake,* pp. 301 ff.

quality command respect and admiration. Who can fail to recognise the force, if not necessarily the truth, of his doctrine about the nature and function of art as we find it stated in a passage written at the end of his life, and which can almost be regarded as his intellectual testament:

A Poet, a Painter, a Musician, an Architect: the Man Or Woman who is not one of these is not a Christian.

You must leave Father and Mother and Houses and Lands if they stand in the way of Art.

Prayer is the Study of Art.

Praise is the Practice of Art.

Fasting etc., all relate to Art.

The outward Ceremony is Antichrist.

The Eternal Body of Man is The Imagination, that is, God himself, The Divine Body, Jesus: we are his Members.

It manifests itself in his Works of Art (In Eternity All is Vision).[19]

[19] *Works,* p. 765.

Appendix A

THE MEANING OF *PITT* AND *NELSON*

BLAKE SUPPLIES the clues to the true meaning of these complicated allegories in the full titles which he gave them in his *Descriptive Catalogue*. The *Nelson* (Plate 46d) he describes as follows: "The spiritual form of Nelson guiding Leviathan, in whose wreathings are infolded the Nations of the Earth";[1] and the *Pitt* (Plate 46c), more elaborately: "The spiritual form of Pitt, guiding Behemoth; he is that Angel who, pleased to perform the Almighty's orders, rides on the whirlwind, directing the storms of war: He is ordering the Reaper to reap the Vine of the Earth, and the Plowman to Plow up the Cities and Towers."[2] The central theme of the *Pitt* is, therefore, War, and if we recall the passage in *Jerusalem*:

> Leviathan
> And Behemoth, the War by Sea enormous and the War
> By Land astounding[3]

we can be sure that the *Nelson* deals with the same subject.

Blake, as we know, hated war, believing only in "Mental Fight"; and in 1808, when these paintings were executed, he had ample reason to feel seriously on the subject, for the Napoleonic Wars were just reaching a new pitch of horror in the opening Peninsular campaign. We must not, however, regard these two paintings as mere protests against these events. Though Blake loathed war, he considered it as a necessary part of the divine plan. His view of it was apocalyptic; for him war was the last stage in the triumph of evil, and the immediate preliminary to the Last Judgement and the final destruction of evil.

[1] *Works,* p. 780.   [2] *Ibid.,* p. 781.   [3] *Ibid.,* p. 38.

Blake conceived of war as a perversion of energy. Energy is in itself good, but it is perverted by man's selfishness.[4] This selfishness is expressed by the rejection of forgiveness, as taught by Christ, in favour of justice or revenge, the doctrine of the materialists,[5] in which category Blake includes not only his immediate enemies like the Deists,[6] but also all tyrants and all those who preach the worldly Christianity of the established churches.[7] It is because of these enemies of the true doctrine of Christ that man's energy, which should be expended in the creation of works of art—for Blake every Christian was an artist —is turned into the paths of destruction and war.

War is, however, the prelude to the Last Judgement. Blake believed that the Last Judgement comes when error reaches its full manifestation, is therefore recognised, and can so be destroyed. War is one form of this manifestation. But there is an even more precise connection between war and the Last Judgement in some of the symbols which Blake uses in describing it. In the title for the *Pitt*, for instance, Blake speaks of war as involving the reaping of the "Vine of the Earth"; and in *Milton,* after a reference to the wine-press of Los, he says: "This Wine-press is call'd War on Earth."[8] Both these ideas—vintage and wine-press—are allusions to the Apocalypse, where the angel is told to "gather the clusters of the vine of the earth" and to "cast it into the great wine-press of the

---

4   And the two Sources of Life in Eternity, Hunting and War,
    Are become the two Sources of dark and bitter Death and of corroding Hell
    (*Works*, p. 632).

The same idea is repeated in *Milton* (*ibid.*, p. 533) and in *The Four Zoas:* "For war is energy Enslaved" (*ibid.*, p. 429).

5   Why should Punishment Weave the Veil with Iron Wheels of War
    When Forgiveness might it Weave with Wings of Cherubim? (*ibid.*, p. 591).

6 The principal attack on the Deists as the cause of war is contained in the address which prefaces the third book of *Jerusalem* (*ibid.*, pp. 646 ff.); but it is also referred to in *Milton* (*ibid.*, p. 504).

7 Tyrants and the creators of established religion are classed together in a passage in *Milton*:

    Abraham, Moses, Solomon, Paul, Constantine, Charlemaine,
    Luther, these seven are the Male-Females, the Dragon Forms,
    Religion hid in War, a Dragon red and hidden Harlot (*ibid.*, p. 539).

8 *Ibid.*, p. 516.

wrath of God."[9] This action immediately precedes the pouring out of the plagues, the darkest stage in the whole book, which in its turn is a prelude to the fall of Babylon and the Last Judgement proper. In Blake the position of the vintage is the same. It is the last stage in the triumph of evil before its final destruction.

This conception of war is implicit in the paintings which we are considering, and when we study them in detail we see that they are full of symbols from the Apocalypse and allusions to Blake's own doctrines about the Last Judgement.

Of the two the *Pitt* is by far the more complicated. Pitt himself stands in the centre, poised on the back of Behemoth. With one hand he holds a light rein with which he guides the monster, and with the other he points downwards towards a stream at his feet. Through the skin of Behemoth we can see the shadowy forms of the kings and tyrants of the earth which have been swallowed up by the monster, and all around and above it are figures of men in attitudes of terror. Behind the central figure on the left is a man holding a sickle, to the right a man driving a plough through the earth. Above are six circles containing figures which cannot be completely identified owing to the damaged state of the painting.[10]

All the symbols in this painting appear in poems Blake composed at about the time that the painting was executed (1808). The last Night of *The Four Zoas* (finished in 1804), the whole of *Milton* (1804–8), and parts of *Jerusalem* (begun 1808) deal with the Last Judgement and the events which lead up to it, and from them we can explain Blake's meaning in his composition. But the task is not easy, since the poet is not always consistent in his use of symbols, and certain details admit of more than one interpretation.

The main points, however, are clear. Pitt, who is of course only the representative of a spiritual state and has little connection with what we should call the "real" Pitt, is the angel "directing the storms of war." It is he who is in charge of the whole scene and who directs the activities of the other actors so that the Last Judgement shall ensue. Now in *Milton* it is Los, the embodiment

[9] Revelation 14.18–19.
[10] The painting was restored by George Richmond while in the possession of Samuel Palmer (see Butlin, *Catalogue*, p. 54).

of poetry and the spiritual life and the hero of many of Blake's epics, who performs the function.[11] And it is not, I think, fanciful to regard Pitt in the painting as a new personification for Los. Moreover, Los is always associated with the element of Earth, and it will be remembered that Blake, in the lines quoted above from *Jerusalem,* defines Behemoth, the monster on which Pitt stands, as the symbol of war on land, as opposed to war by sea. Why Blake should have chosen this particular character to stand for Los is not clear, but his association of qualities with real people and places is often obscure and, without the help of other references, cannot always be explained.[12] The function of Pitt-Los is further indicated by the only one of the scenes depicted on his halo which is decipherable. This shows an old man holding a scroll in his outstretched hands and seems to represent the verse of the Apocalypse which says: "And the heaven departed as a scroll when it is rolled together," [13] a subject which Blake depicts in similar form in his *Death on the Pale Horse,* except that the scroll is there rolled up by an angel, not by an old man.

The two figures in the background present certain difficulties in interpretation. The man holding the sickle appears to be Urizen, the embodiment of rationalism and materialism. For a passage in the *Four Zoas* describes his action in the painting, even to the gesture of taking the sickle down from among the stars:

> Then Urizen arose and took his sickle in his hand.
> There is a brazen sickle, and a scythe of iron hid
> Deep in the South, guarded by a few solitary stars.
> This sickle Urizen took; and the scythe his sons embrac'd
> And went forth and began to reap; and all his joyful sons
> Reap'd the wide Universe and bound in sheaves a wondrous harvest.[14]

---

[11] *Works,* p. 511.

[12] The only direct reference to Pitt, which occurs in a letter of 1801 (*Works,* p. 1057), does not advance matters much: "Bacon and Newton would prescribe ways of making the world heavier to me, and Pitt would prescribe distress for a medicinal potion; but as none on Earth can give me Mental Distress, and I know that all Distress inflicted by Heaven is a Mercy, a Fig for all Corporeal!" This passage at least shows that Blake associated Pitt with an "Eternal state" as he did Bacon and Newton. The puzzling feature is that he should associate a man whom he must have hated as the prosecutor of wars with Los, the symbol of energy and imagination; but in their particular apocalyptic function the two figures can be regarded as related, since war is energy perverted.

[13] Revelation 6.14; see also *Works,* p. 423.　　　　[14] *Works,* p. 448.

The identification of the ploughman, however, complicates the problem. For he, too, seems to be Urizen, who in another passage from the *Four Zoas* is described in the following way:

> He laid his hand on the Plow,
> Thro' dismal darkness drave the Plow of ages over Cities
> And all their Villages; or Mountains and all their Vallies;
> Over the graves and caverns of the dead; Over the Planets
> And over the void spaces; over sun and moon and star and constellation.[15]

It is possible that Blake intended to represent the two successive actions of Urizen as simultaneous—a practice which would not be contrary to his principles—but, if this is so, it is surprising that he makes the two figures so different in appearance. The man with the sickle has, for instance, long fair hair, whereas the ploughman has short, dark, curly hair. We must, therefore, examine the possibility that these two figures represent other characters, and the only plausible alternative is that they should be Rintrah, or Wrath, and Palamabron, or Pity. Both these characters are closely connected with the events leading up to the Last Judgement, and they appear together in this way in the last lines of *Milton:*

> Rintrah and Palamabron view the Human Harvest beneath.
> Their Wine-presses and Barns stand open, the Ovens are prepared,
> The Waggons ready; terrific Lions and Tygers sport and play.
> All Animals upon the Earth are prepar'd in all their strength
> To go forth to the Great Harvest and Vintage of the Nations.[16]

Lions and tigers are for Blake the symbols of wrath and war, so this passage can be related fairly closely to the painting. We also know that the symbol of Rintrah is the plough, but unfortunately that of Palamabron is usually the harrow, and not the sickle. Nor can we solve the problem by taking the man with the sickle as Urizen and the ploughman as Rintrah, since these two characters are not of the same order—Urizen is one of the four Zoas, and Rintrah is one of the sons of Los. The matter must, therefore, be left in doubt.

In the poems of Blake to which we have referred the reaping and ploughing are preludes to the pressing of the grapes in the wine-presses of Luvah, the Zoa who represents the emotions. This does not actually appear in the painting, but

[15] *Ibid.,* p. 436.   [16] *Ibid.,* p. 549.

below the feet of Pitt-Los, and just behind Behemoth, there is a stream towards which Pitt-Los points. This appears to be the stream which flows from the wine-presses:

> the wine-presses were filled;
> The blood of life flow'd plentiful.[17]

In the foreground, is the monster Behemoth itself, in which are swallowed up the tyrants of the earth. It is a regular feature of Blake's descriptions of the Last Judgement that the oppressed should rise up and destroy their rulers; but here, since it is Behemoth that has devoured them, we must suppose that Blake imagined that they would be destroyed by war itself.

There is much in this painting that is still obscure, but the companion piece presents fewer difficulties. Blake's own description covers the essential points, and we need only point out that he has illustrated the words "the Nations of the Earth" by introducing a black man in the foreground as well as the various European figures.

One problem, however, should be considered. If Pitt is Los, does Nelson also represent one of Blake's abstractions? The answer seems to be that Nelson stands for Tharmas, the one Zoa whom we have not so far encountered. Los, we have seen, stands for the Spirit; Luvah for the Emotions, Urizen for Reason; and Tharmas is the symbol of the Senses. His connection with Nelson and sea warfare is first suggested by the fact that he is associated with the element of Water. But two passages in the *Four Zoas* make the connection even closer:

> Then Tharmas took the Winnowing fan; the winnowing wind furious
> Above, veered round by violent whirlwind, driven west and south,
> Tossed the Nations like chaff into the seas of Tharmas.[18]

and:

> In his hand Tharmas takes the storms: he turns the whirlwind loose
> Upon the wheels; the stormy seas howl at his dread command.[19]

This description suits the attitude of Nelson, who, it will be noticed, even holds a thunderbolt—the storms—in his hand.[20]

---

[17] *Ibid.*, p. 454.   [18] *Ibid.*, p. 451.   [19] *Ibid.*, p. 458.
[20] I find it quite impossible to follow David Erdman's interpretation of the *Nelson* (*Blake Prophet against Empire*, pp. 416 ff.). I cannot believe that the lines of radiance

Blake seems to have been much obsessed by the problem of war during the years 1808–9. Two other paintings in the exhibition of 1809 deal with this theme. In *The Bard,* from Gray, the destruction of the Welsh bards by the invading English armies must have meant for Blake—as for Gray—the destruction of poetry by war in general. *The Ancient Britons,* now lost, seems to have been somewhat more obscure, but from Blake's account of it we know that it depicted the last battle of Arthur, in which only three men survived: "The Strongest Man, the Beautifullest Man, and the Ugliest Man." Here the note is more optimistic, for Blake says that the ancient Britons "were overwhelmed by brutal arms, all but a small remnant; Strength, Beauty and Ugliness escaped the wreck, and remain for ever unsubdued, age after age." [21]

The theme recurs in the water-colour of *The Whore of Babylon* (dated 1809), in which, below the gigantic figure of the woman, Blake has shown a series of tiny figures, all of which are engaged in fighting. This is strictly in accordance with the symbolism which he attaches to Babylon in his poems where she is described as "Mystery" and is the root of all false religion and, therefore, war. Her destruction is one of the recurrent themes in his account of the Last Judgement. Certain of the biblical water-colours for Butts also bear on similar themes. These illustrate chapters 12 and 13 of the Revelation with the story of the Red Dragon and the Woman clothed with the Sun and, in passing, the war between Michael and Satan.[22] Here again the principal idea is the destruction of mankind by war and other horrors as a prelude to the Harvest of the World, which is described in chapter 14.

---

round the central figure are really thunderbolts directed at him; nor that what he holds in his right hand is the hair that he has torn from the figure floating above him, which on this interpretation would symbolise France shorn of her sea power at Trafalgar. Above all, the figure in the jaws of Leviathan cannot be Christ, as Mr. Erdman proposes. It is inconceivable that Blake should represent Christ in this degrading pose and with so evil a face, and, whatever it is that he wears in his hair, it is certainly not a Crown of Thorns.

[21] *Works,* p. 795.

[22] These are Nos. 163 and 167 in Keynes. The subject of No. 163a is wrongly identified; it represents chapter 12, verses 14–16, and not, like 163b, verses 1–4.

Appendix B

SUBJECTS OF BIBLICAL PAINTINGS EXECUTED BY BLAKE FOR THOMAS BUTTS

THIS APPENDIX contains lists of two biblical series of works made by Blake for Thomas Butts, the first executed in tempera in the year 1799–1800, the second and larger series in water-colours, probably executed between 1800 and 1805.

These works are all recorded in *Blake's Illustrations to the Bible,* edited by Geoffrey Keynes, and the parenthetical references are to this work. The titles are listed specially here because there is reason to believe (pp. 64 ff., 69 ff.) that Blake planned these groups as continuous series developing a personal religious idea.

The Tempera Series, 1799–1800

Lot and his Daughter (Keynes, 22)
Abraham and Isaac (Keynes, 23)
Moses Placed in the Ark of Bulrushes (Keynes, 33)
Samson Pulling down the Temple (Keynes, 53)
Bathsheba (Keynes, 60)
The Judgement of Solomon (Keynes, 62)
Esther (Keynes, 66)
Susanna and the Elders (Keynes, 85)
The Angel Gabriel Appearing to Zacharias (Keynes, 90)
The Nativity (Keynes, 91)

The Circumcision (Keynes, 92)

The Adoration of the Kings (Keynes, 93; dated 1799)

The Flight into Egypt (Keynes, 95; the date is difficult to read but is probably 1799)

The Riposo (Keynes, 96)

The Silenzio (Keynes, 99)

The Infant Jesus Riding on a Lamb (Keynes, 100; dated 1800)

The Christ Child Asleep on a Cross (Keynes, 101)

The Christ Child Taught to Read (Keynes, 106; dated 1799)

Christ with the Doctors in the Temple (Keynes, 107)

The Baptism of Christ (Keynes, 109)

Christ Raising Jairus' Daughter (Keynes, 113)

The Pool of Bethesda (Keynes, 116)

Christ Blessing the little Children (Keynes, 120; dated 1799)

Christ Giving Sight to the Blind Man (Keynes, 124)

Christ's Entry into Jerusalem (Keynes, 129)

The Last Supper (Keynes, 132)

The Agony in the Garden (Keynes, 134)

The Procession from Calvary (Keynes, 142)

The Entombment (Keynes, 143)

Christ and St. Thomas (Keynes, 152)

Faith, Hope, and Charity (Keynes, 158; dated 1799)

Christ the Mediator (Keynes, 171)

These are all of more or less identical format. In addition there were five upright compositions:

Moses Indignant at the Golden Calf (Keynes, 42)

The Four Evangelists (Keynes, 86–89; one dated 1799).

Rossetti mentions two further tempera paintings belonging to Butts which, according to him, were dated 1799 and for which he tentatively suggests the titles: *The Sons of God Saw the Daughters of Men* (Keynes, 18), and *Rachel Giving Joseph the Coat of Many Colours* (Keynes, 27).

The Water-Colour Series, ca. 1800–1805

The list is not complete, because some compositions mentioned by Rossetti as belonging to Butts cannot now be identified, and, since it is impossible to determine whether they were water-colours or tempera, they have been omitted.

The Creation of Light (Keynes, 1)
God Blessing the Seventh Day (Keynes, 2)
God Bringing Eve to Adam (Keynes, 6)
The Angel of the Divine Presence Clothing Adam and Eve (Keynes, 11; 1803)
Noah Sacrificing (Keynes, 20)
Jacob's Ladder (Keynes, 25; exhibited at the Royal Academy in 1808 and in
   Blake's exhibition in 1809)
Jacob and His Twelve Sons (Keynes, 26)
Joseph and Potiphar's Wife (Keynes, 28)
The Finding of Moses (Keynes, 35)
Moses and the Burning Bush (Keynes, 36)
Famine (Keynes, 37; 1805)
Plague (Keynes, 38c)
Pestilence (The Death of the First-born) (Keynes, 39)
Moses Striking the Rock (Keynes, 44; 1805)
The Brazen Serpent (Keynes, 45)
God Writing upon the Tablets of the Covenant (Keynes, 46)
The Burial of Moses (Keynes, 47)
The Stoning of Achan (Keynes, 48)
Jephthah Met by His Daughter (Keynes, 49)
The Sacrifice of Jephthah's Daughter (Keynes, 50)
Samson Breaking His Bonds (Keynes, 51)
Samson Subdued (Keynes, 52)
Ruth and Naomi (Keynes, 54; 1803; shown in Blake's exhibition in 1809)
David and Goliath (Keynes, 55)
The Ghost of Samuel Appearing to Saul (Keynes, 58)
The Pardon of Absalom (Keynes, 61)

The Man of God and Jeroboam (Keynes, 63)

God Answering Job out of the Whirlwind (Keynes, 71)

David Delivered out of Many Waters (Keynes, 75)

Christ Girding Himself with Strength (Keynes, 76)

Mercy and Truth Are Met Together (Keynes, 77)

By the Waters of Babylon (Keynes, 78)

The King of Babylon in Hell (Keynes, 79)

Ezekiel's Vision (Keynes, 80)

Satan in His Original Glory (Keynes, 82)

Presentation of Christ in the Temple (Keynes, 94)

The Riposo (Keynes, 96b; 1806)

Christ in the Lap of Truth (Keynes, 104)

The Christ Child Saying his Prayers (Keynes, 105)

Christ in the Carpenter's Shop (Keynes, 108)

Baptism (Keynes, 109b)

The Third Temptation (Keynes, 110)

Christ Baptizing (Keynes, 111; 1805)

Healing of the Woman with the Bloody Issue (Keynes, 112)

The Miracle of the Loaves and Fishes (Keynes, 117)

The Transfiguration (Keynes, 119)

The Widow of Nain (Keynes, 121)

The Woman Taken in Adultery (Keynes, 123)

The Raising of Lazarus (Keynes, 125)

Mary Magdalene Washing the Feet of Christ (Keynes, 126)

Christ in the House of Martha and Mary (Keynes, 127)

The Wise and Foolish Virgins (Keynes, 130)

Christ Accompanied by Figures with Musical Instruments (Keynes, 133)

The Betrayal (Keynes, 135)

Christ Crowned with Thorns (Keynes, 137)

The King of the Jews (Keynes, 138)

The Soldiers Casting Lots (Keynes, 139; 1800; shown in Blake's exhibition, 1809)

Crucifixion (Keynes, 140)

Crucifixion (Keynes, 141)

The Entombment (Keynes, 144)

The Sealing of the Sepulchre (Keynes, 145)

Angels Hovering over the Body of Jesus (Keynes, 146; exhibited at the Royal Academy in 1808 and in Blake's exhibition, 1809)

The Angel Rolling the Stone from the Sepulchre (Keynes, 147)

Resurrection (Keynes, 148)

The Three Marys at the Sepulchre (Keynes, 149; 1803)

Christ Appearing to the Magdalene (Keynes, 150)

The Ascension (Keynes, 153)

The Conversion of Saul (Keynes, 154)

St. Paul Preaching in Athens (Keynes, 155; 1803)

St. Paul before Felix (Keynes, 156)

St. Paul and the Viper (two versions) (Keynes, 157)

Seven Golden Candlesticks (Keynes, 159)

Four-and-Twenty Elders Casting Down Their Crowns (Keynes, 160)

Death on the Pale Horse (Keynes, 161)

The Angel of the Revelation (Keynes, 162)

The Great Dragon (two versions) (Keynes, 163)

Michael and Satan (Keynes, 164)

The Devil Is Come Down (Keynes, 165)

Power Was Given Him Over All Nations (Keynes, 166)

The Beast (Keynes, 167)

The River of Life (Keynes, 170)

The Death of St. Joseph (Keynes, 172; 1803)

The Death of the Virgin (Keynes, 173; 1803)

The Assumption of the Virgin (Keynes, 174; 1806).

Plates

Plate 1. GLAD DAY. COLOURED PRINT

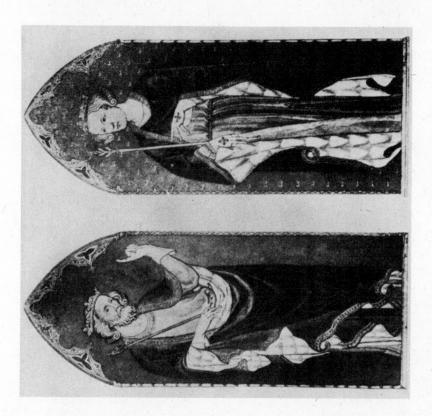

Plate 2a. KING SEBERT AND KING HENRY III

b. AVELINE, COUNTESS OF LANCASTER

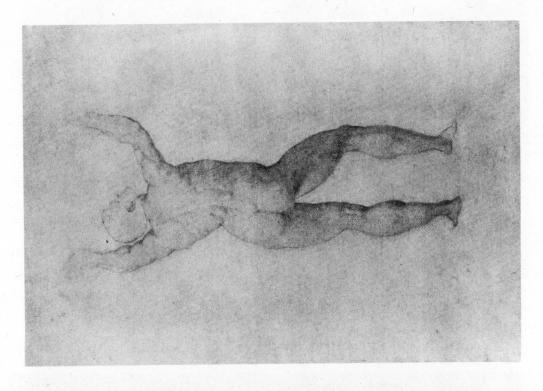

Plate 3a. ENGRAVING AFTER MICHELANGELO. FIRST STATE

b. NUDE

Plate 4*a*. THE PENANCE OF JANE SHORE

b. THE ORDEAL OF QUEEN EMMA

Plate *5a.* EDWARD AND ELEANOR
   b. EDWARD AND ELEANOR, BY ANGELICA KAUFFMANN

Plate 6a and b. ROMAN BRONZE, HERCULANEUM. BACK AND FRONT VIEWS

c. DRAWING BY BLAKE

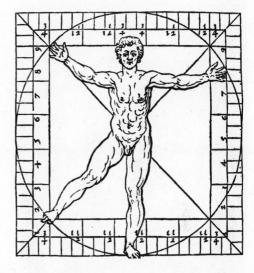

Plate 7a. GLAD DAY. ENGRAVING. *b*. PROPORTION DIAGRAM, FROM SCAMOZZI

c. GLAD DAY. DRAWING

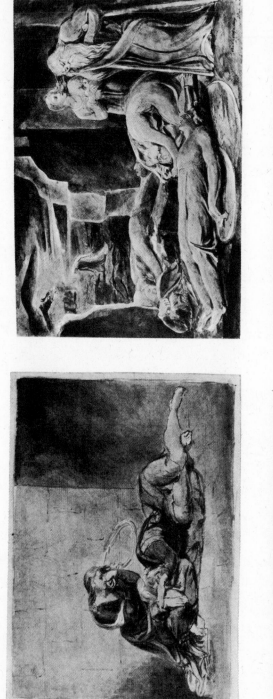

Plate 8a. LEAR AND CORDELIA. *b.* THE BREACH IN THE CITY
c. JOSEPH AND HIS BRETHREN. *d.* THE TRIUMPH OF THE THAMES, BY BARRY

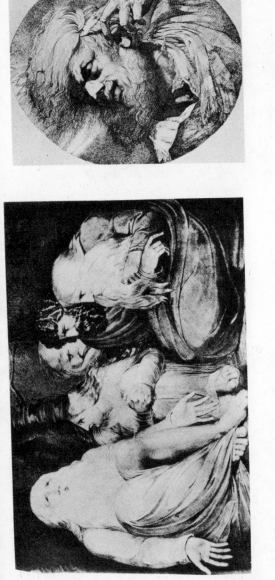

Plate 9a. THE COMPLAINT OF JOB. *b.* KING LEAR, BY MORTIMER
c. JOB REPROVED BY HIS FRIENDS, BY BARRY. *d.* KING LEAR

Plate 10a. SATAN, SIN AND DEATH, BY STOTHARD b. SATAN, SIN AND DEATH, BY BARRY
c. SATAN, SIN AND DEATH, BY FUSELI

Plate *11a*. SATAN, SIN AND DEATH. *b*. RICHARD III AND THE GHOSTS

c. RICHARD III AND THE GHOSTS, BY FUSELI

Plate *12a*. FRONTISPIECE TO COMMINS' *Elegy Set to Music*. *b.* ILLUSTRATION TO OSSIAN, BY STOTHARD
c. MACBETH AND THE GHOST OF BANQUO

Plate 13a. LADY MACBETH AND DUNCAN. b. LADY MACBETH SLEEPWALKING, BY FUSELI
c. MACBETH AND THE GHOST OF BANQUO, BY ROMNEY

Plate 14a. TITLE PAGE TO *Songs of Innocence*
b. TITLE PAGE TO *Songs of Experience*

Plate 15a. INFANT JOY, FROM *Songs of Innocence*

b. THE SICK ROSE, FROM *Songs of Experience*

Plate 16a. INTRODUCTION TO *Songs of Innocence*

Plate 17a. ILLUSTRATION TO MARMONTEL, *Adelaïde*, BY STOTHARD

b. THE SHEPHERD, FROM *Songs of Innocence*

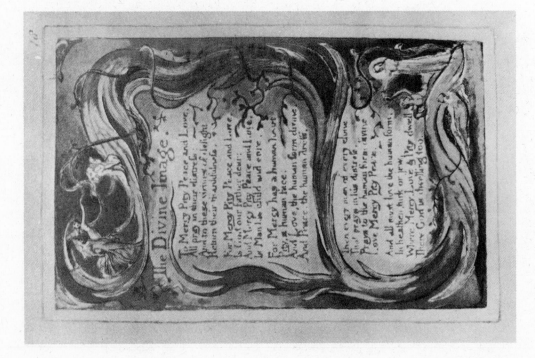

Plate 18a. THE DIVINE IMAGE, FROM *Songs of Innocence*

b. THE BLOSSOM, FROM *Songs of Innocence*

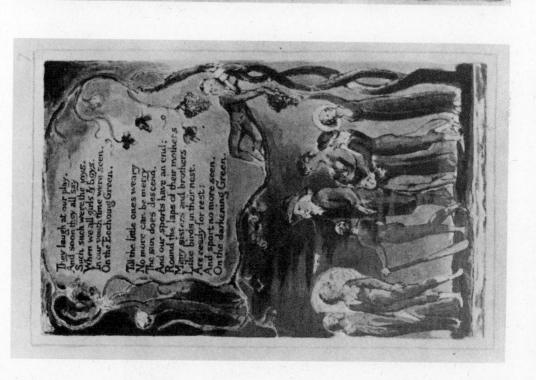

Plate 19a. THE ECCHOING GREEN, FROM *Songs of Innocence*

b. HOLY THURSDAY, FROM *Songs of Innocence*

Plate 20a. THEL AND THE WORM
  b. PLATE FROM *Visions of the Daughters of Albion*

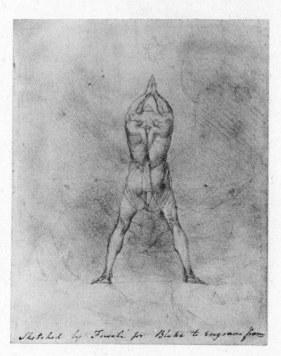

Plate 21a. THE NILE, BY FUSELI. b. THE NILE, BY BLAKE AFTER FUSELI

c. THE SPIRIT OF GOD FLOATING OVER CHAOS, BY ROMNEY

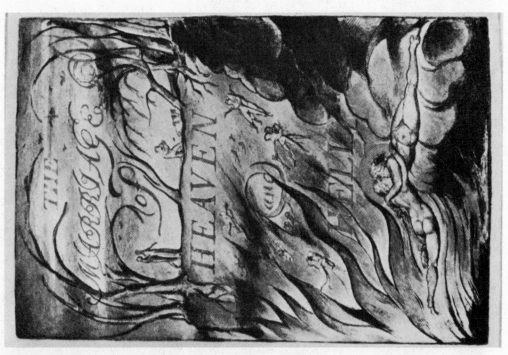

Plate 22a. TITLE PAGE TO *The Marriage of Heaven and Hell*
b. TITLE PAGE TO *Visions of the Daughters of Albion*

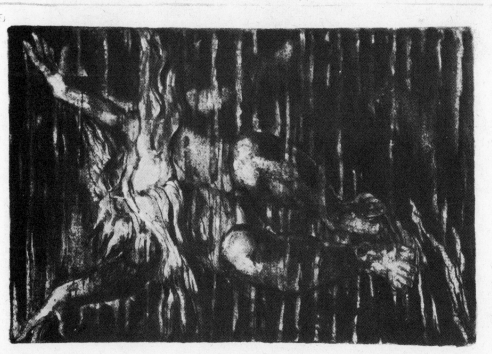

Plate 23a. URIZEN SUNK IN THE WATERS OF MATERIALISM, FROM *The Book of Urizen*

b. PLAGUE, FROM *Europe*

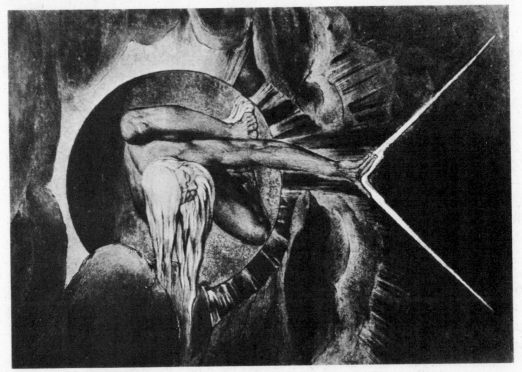

Plate 24a. THE ANCIENT OF DAYS

b. THE CREATION, FROM 13TH-CENTURY MANUSCRIPT

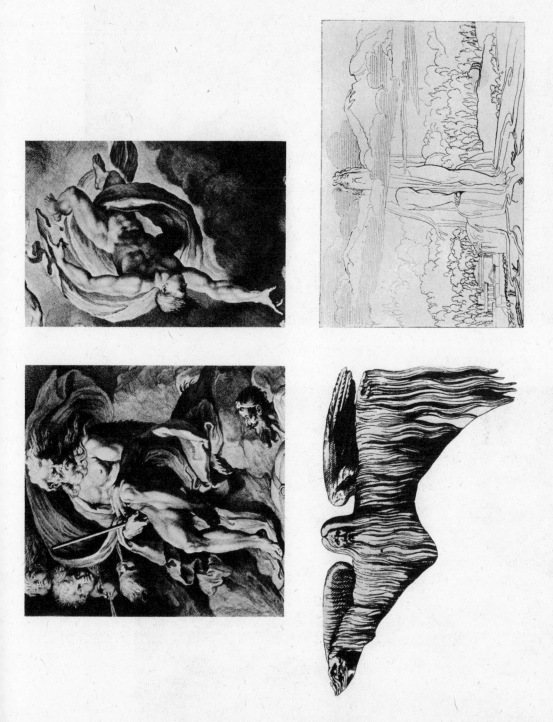

Plate 25a. NEPTUNE, BY TIBALDI. *b.* FIGURE, BY TIBALDI
c. JUPITER PLUVIUS, ROMAN RELIEF. *d.* ILLUSTRATION TO DANTE, BY FLAXMAN

Plate 26a. HECATE

      b. GOD CREATING ADAM

Plate 27a. THE LAZAR HOUSE

b. THE LAZAR HOUSE, BY FUSELI

Plate 28a. PITY
     b. ELIJAH

Plate 29a. PITY. DRAWING
b. PITY. DRAWING

Plate 30a. ABIAS, BY GHISI AFTER MICHELANGELO. *b.* ABIAS, BY BLAKE AFTER GHISI
c. NEWTON

Plate 31a. DEATH ON THE PALE HORSE, BY MORTIMER. *b.* NEBUCHADNEZZAR, BY MORTIMER.

c. NEBUCHADNEZZAR

Plate 32a. GOOD AND EVIL ANGELS. WATER-COLOUR. *b.* GOOD AND EVIL ANGELS. COLOUR-PRINT

c. DRAWING, BY FLAXMAN. *d.* GOD APPEARING TO ISAAC, BY RAPHAEL

Plate 33. THE PROCESSION FROM CALVARY

Plate 34a. BATHSHEBA

b. CHRIST THE MEDIATOR

Plate *35a*. THE CHRIST CHILD ASLEEP ON THE CROSS

      b. THE NATIVITY

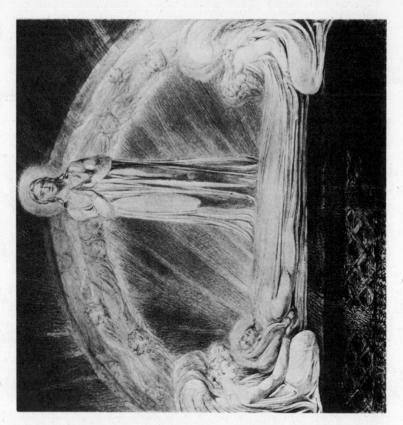

Plate 37a. THE SOLDIERS CASTING LOTS FOR CHRIST'S RAIMENT

b. CHRIST IN THE SEPULCHRE

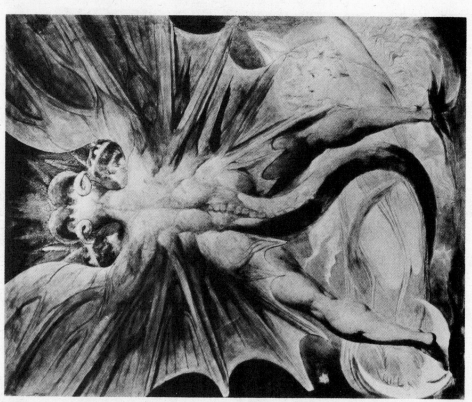

Plate 38a. THE RED DRAGON AND THE WOMAN CLOTHED WITH THE SUN

b. THE RIVER OF LIFE

Plate 39a. ST. MICHAEL BINDING THE DRAGON

b. INITIAL, FROM THE WINCHESTER BIBLE, 12TH-CENTURY MANUSCRIPT

Plate 40a. PESTILENCE. *b.* DAVID AND GOLIATH. *c.* ACHILLES AT THE PYRE OF PATROCLUS, BY FUSELI

Plate 41a. HAMLET AND THE GHOST OF HIS FATHER, BY FUSELI
b. VORTIGERN AND ROWENA, BY MORTIMER. C. HAMLET AND THE GHOST OF HIS FATHER

Plate 42a. GOD BLESSING THE SEVENTH DAY. *b.* BOSS, FROM YORK MINSTER. *c.* ILLUSTRATION TO MILTON, *Ode on the Morning of Christ's Nativity. d.* ILLUSTRATION TO THE BOOK OF ENOCH

Plate 43a. CHRIST IN GLORY, BY PONTORMO. b. DAVID AND NATHAN, BY SALVIATI. c. MY SON! MY SON! FROM *The Gates of Paradise*. d. DAVID AND SAUL, BY SALVIATI

Plate 44. JACOB'S DREAM

Plate 45. ADAM AND EVE ASLEEP

Plate 46a. THE CREATION OF EVE. DRAWING. b. THE CREATION OF EVE. WATER-COLOUR

c. PITT GUIDING BEHEMOTH. d. NELSON GUIDING LEVIATHAN

Plate 47. ADAM AND EVE WITH RAPHAEL

Plate 48a. ALBION AND THE CRUCIFIED CHRIST, FROM *Jerusalem*

Plate 49a. THE SOUL REUNITED WITH GOD, FROM *Jerusalem*

b. THE PRODIGAL SON, BY MARTIN DE VOS

Plate 50a. HUMAN-HEADED BULL, PERSEPOLIS. *b.* CHARIOT WITH HUMAN-HEADED BULLS, FROM *Jerusalem*
c. AN INDIAN DEITY, FROM MOOR, *Hindu Pantheon. d.* BEULAH ENTHRONED ON A SUNFLOWER,
FROM *Jerusalem*

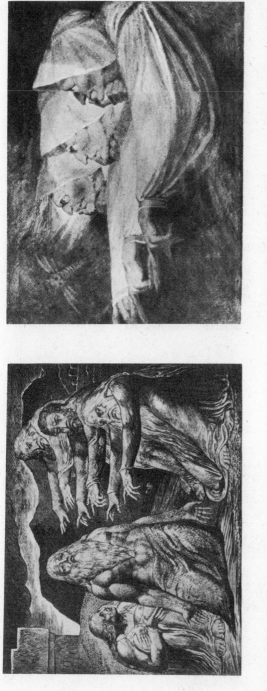

Plate 51a. JOB MOCKED, ILLUSTRATION TO THE BOOK OF JOB *b.* THE THREE WITCHES, BY FUSELI
c. THE THREE ACCUSERS, FROM *Jerusalem. d.* THE FALL OF THE GIANTS, ENGRAVING AFTER PERINO DEL VAGA

Plate 52. ILLUSTRATIONS TO THE BOOK OF JOB. *a.* JOB IN PROSPERITY

b. THE DESTRUCTION OF JOB'S SONS AND DAUGHTERS

Plate 53. ILLUSTRATIONS TO THE BOOK OF JOB. *a.* "THEN A SPIRIT PASSED BEFORE MY FACE"

b. THE MORNING STARS SINGING TOGETHER

Plate 54a. RELIEF, PERSEPOLIS. *b.* ILLUSTRATION TO YOUNG, *Night Thoughts*
c. THE ANGEL OF THE APOCALYPSE, FROM 13TH-CENTURY MANUSCRIPT

Plate 55a. SATAN SMITING JOB. ENGRAVING

b. SATAN SMITING JOB. TEMPERA PAINTING

Plate 56a. THE SPEECH OF ELIHU. ENGRAVING
b. THE SPEECH OF ELIHU. WATER-COLOUR

 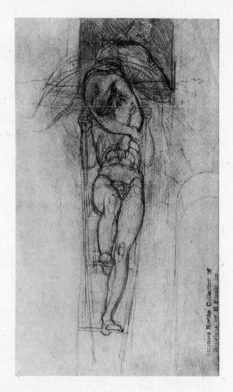

Plate 57a. FAINTING WOMAN, BY FUSELI. b. ROMEO AND JULIET, BY FUSELI

c. THE DEATH OF ABEL

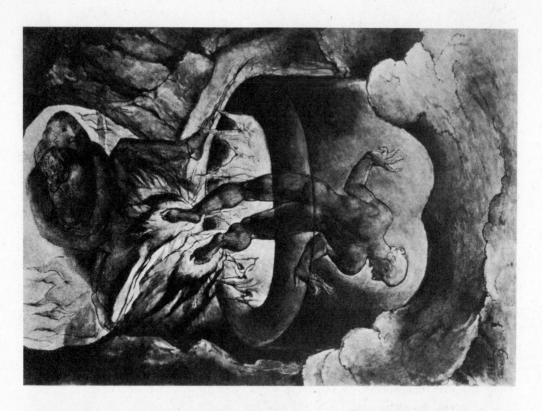

Plate 58. ILLUSTRATIONS TO DANTE. *a*. HELL GATE
b. THE SIMONIAC POPE

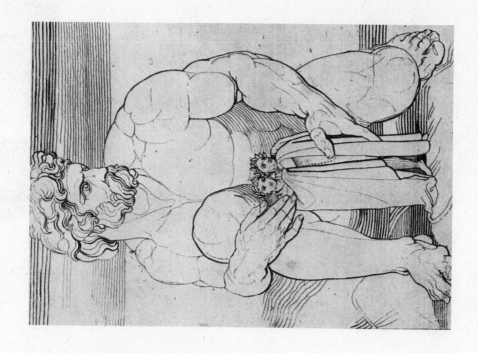

Plate 59. ILLUSTRATIONS TO DANTE. *a.* ANTAEUS
b. ANTAEUS, BY FLAXMAN

Plate 60. ILLUSTRATIONS TO DANTE. *a.* THE CIRCLE OF THE LUSTFUL

　　b. LUCIA CARRYING DANTE IN HIS SLEEP

Plate *61*. ILLUSTRATIONS TO DANTE. *a*. CAIAPHAS AND THE HYPOCRITES

b. CAIAPHAS AND THE HYPOCRITES, BY FLAXMAN

Plate 62. BEATRICE ON THE CAR, ILLUSTRATION TO DANTE

Plate 63. BEATRICE ADDRESSING DANTE FROM THE CAR, ILLUSTRATION TO DANTE

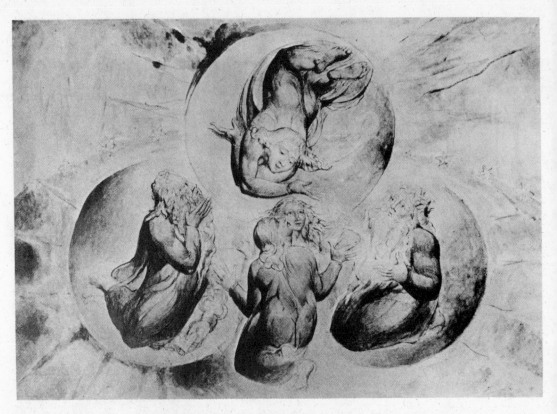

Plate 64a. DANTE AND VIRGIL WITH SAINTS PETER, JAMES AND JOHN, ILLUSTRATION TO DANTE

b. INITIAL, FROM PSALTER, 13TH-CENTURY MANUSCRIPT

Bibliography

THE LITERATURE on Blake is vast, and the following list is intended to include only those works which give a useful general account of his life and ideas or are particularly concerned with his painting and engraving.

The most complete edition of Blake's works is that in three volumes edited by Geoffrey Keynes and published by the Nonesuch Press in 1925. References in the present book are to the small one-volume edition edited by the same hand and published by the same Press in 1927.

The Blake Trust is engaged in publishing facsimiles of Blake's works. So far the *Songs of Innocence and Experience,* the *Book of Urizen,* and *Jerusalem* have appeared, and the *Marriage of Heaven and Hell* will be ready shortly.

The principal exhibitions of Blake's works are listed in M. Butlin, *A Catalogue of the Works of William Blake in the Tate Gallery* (London, 1957). To his list should be added the two important exhibitions held in the United States, the first in the Philadelphia Museum of Art in 1939, the second in the National Gallery, Washington, D.C., in 1957.

Barry, James. The Works of James Barry. London, 1809.

Binyon, L. The Drawings and Engravings of William Blake. London, 1922.

—— The Engraved Designs of William Blake. London, 1926.

Binyon, L., and G. Keynes. Blake's Illustrations to the Book of Job. New York, 1935.

Blunt, A. "Blake's *Ancient of Days:* The Symbolism of the Compasses," *Journal of the Warburg Institute,* II (1938), 53 ff.

Blunt, A. "Blake's *Glad Day*," *Journal of the Warburg Institute*, II (1938), 65 ff.

—— "Blake's *Brazen Serpent*," *Journal of the Warburg and Courtauld Institutes*, VI (1943), 225 ff.

—— "Blake's Pictorial Imagination," *Journal of the Warburg and Courtauld Institutes*, VI (1943), 190 ff.

—— Introduction to *A Catalogue of the Works of William Blake in the Tate Gallery*. London, 1957.

Boase, T. S. R. "An Extra-Illustrated Second Folio of Shakespeare," *British Museum Quarterly*, XX (1955), 4 ff.

Bronowski, J. William Blake, a Man without a Mask. London, 1947.

Brown, A. R. "Blake's Drawings for the Book of Enoch," *Burlington Magazine*, LXXVII (1940), 80 ff.

Bryant, J. A New System, or, analysis of Antient Mythology. London, 1774.

Burke, E. Philosophical Enquiry into the Origin of Our Ideas of the Sublime and the Beautiful, ed. by J. T. Boulton. London, 1958.

Butlin, M. A Catalogue of the Works of William Blake in the Tate Gallery. London, 1957.

Collins Baker, C. "The Sources of Blake's Pictorial Expression," *Huntington Library Quarterly*, IV (1941), 359 f.

Coxhead, A. C. Thomas Stothard. London, 1906.

Crookshank, A. "The Drawings of George Romney," *Burlington Magazine*, XCIX (1957), 42 ff.

Damon, S. F. William Blake: His Philosophy and Symbols. Boston and New York, 1924.

Erdman, D. Blake: Prophet against Empire. Princeton, 1954.

Figgis, D. The Paintings of William Blake. London, 1925.

Flaxman, J. Lectures on Sculpture. London, 1838.

Frye, N. Fearful Symmetry: A Study of William Blake. Princeton, 1947.

Gilchrist, A. The Life of William Blake. 1st ed., London, 1863. Republished with Rossetti's list of Blake's works and an introduction by W. Graham Robertson, London, 1907. In the present work references are to the edition by R. Todd, London, 1942.

Gough, R. Sepulchral Monuments in Great Britain. London, 1786–96.

Keynes, G. A Bibliography of William Blake. New York, 1921.

—— Introduction to *The Tempera Paintings of William Blake, a Critical Catalogue*. Arts Council of Great Britain, London, 1951.

Keynes, G., ed. Pencil Drawings by William Blake. London, 1927.

—— The Note-Book of William Blake Called The Rossetti Manuscript. London, 1935.

—— William Blake's Illustrations to the Book of Job. New York, 1935.

—— Blake Studies. London, 1949.

—— William Blake's Engravings. London, 1950.

—— Engravings by William Blake: The Separate Plates. Dublin, 1956.

—— The Letters of William Blake. London, 1956.

—— Blake's Pencil Drawings: Second Series. London, 1956.

—— William Blake's Illustrations to the Bible. London, 1957.

Keynes, G., and E. Wolf. William Blake's Illuminated Books. 2d ed. New York, 1953.

Margoliouth, H. M. "Blake's Drawings for Young's *Night Thoughts*," in *The Divine Vision*, ed. by V. de S. Pinto. London, 1957.

Mengs, A. R. The Works of Anthony Raphael Mengs. London, 1796.

Merchant, W. M. Shakespeare and the Artist. London, 1959.

Nanavutty, P. "A Title-Page in Blake's Illustrated Genesis Manuscript," *Journal of the Warburg and Courtauld Institutes*, X (1947), 114 ff.

Preston, K., ed. The Blake Collection of W. Graham Robertson. London, 1952.

Raine, K. "The Sea of Time and Space," *Journal of the Warburg and Courtauld Institutes*, XX (1957), 318 ff.

Rapin de Thoyras. The History of England, trans. by N. Tindal. 3d ed. London, 1743. 5 vols.

Reynolds, J. The Discourses of Sir Joshua Reynolds, ed. by A. Dobson. Oxford, 1907.

Roe, A. S. Blake's Illustrations to the Divine Comedy. Princeton, 1953.

Rossetti, *see* Gilchrist.

Schiff, G. Zeichnungen von J. H. Füssli. Zurich, 1959.

Selincourt, B. de. William Blake. London, 1909.

Society of Antiquaries. Vetusta Monumenta. London, 1767–1833.

—— Archaeologia. London, 1773–

Symons, A. William Blake. London, 1907.

Todd, R. "The Technique of William Blake's Illuminated Printing," *Print Collector's Quarterly*, XXIX (1948), 25 ff.

Wicksteed, J. Blake's Vision of the Book of Job. London, 1910. Reprinted in 1924.

Wilson, M. The Life of William Blake. London, 1927.

Wood, J. The Origin of Building, or the Plagiarism of the Heathen Detected. Bath, 1741.

Index

Icon Editions